Inside the Therapy Room: A Counsellor's Guide to Couples in Conflict

By

Rachel Hilton

Dedication

This book is dedicated to every couple who has ever sat across from one another in quiet pain, unsure of how they arrived at distance instead of closeness.

To those who were brave enough to speak, to listen, and sometimes simply to stay in the room when it would have been easier to walk away.

And to the therapists who hold space for conflict, vulnerability, and hope, often unseen, often unheard, but always deeply committed to helping others find their way back to connection.

Acknowledgments

This book could not have been written without the countless clients who have trusted the therapy process and allowed their stories, struggles, and breakthroughs to inform my work. While every example in this book has been carefully anonymised and adapted, the emotional truths behind them come straight from the therapy room.

I would like to thank my mentors, and my long-suffering good friend and colleague, who have challenged my thinking, supported my growth, and reminded me that good therapy is never about having all the answers, but about asking the right questions with compassion and integrity.

Thank you to my friends and family for their patience, encouragement, and understanding, particularly during the long hours of writing, reflecting, and revisiting emotionally complex material.

Finally, acknowledgements for the work itself, the therapy room, a place of honesty, discomfort, repair, and profound human courage. It truly is a privilege to witness people at their most vulnerable and to walk alongside them as they navigate conflict, healing, and change.

About The Author

Rachel Hilton is a counsellor and hypnotherapist who works with people of all ages, including children, teenagers, adults, older clients, couples, families, and groups, within a broad and inclusive therapeutic practice.

She has worked in counselling on and off for nearly 20 years and as a hypnotherapist for over six years. Her work is flexible, relational, and deeply human, grounded in the belief that therapy does not come in one neat format. Some people need to talk, some need to move, some need to create, and some simply need a safe space to cry or sit quietly. All of it matters.

Rachel is multi award-winning and finds real satisfaction in helping people notice the patterns they have picked up along the way, understand why those patterns exist, and decide what they want to do differently so that life can feel lighter and freer.

Originally from London, Rachel moved to the Norfolk and Suffolk borders nearly 30 years ago. She is a mother to three grown children and, more recently, to a puppy called Agnes. Her work has continually reinforced her belief that lasting change happens most sustainably when people feel understood, supported, and guided with patience and consistency, rather than rushed or judged.

Contents

Foreword

In a quiet country town in East Anglia, I have spent many years sitting across from couples whose lives have unravelled, twisted, re-stitched or quietly frayed behind closed doors. I have watched people who once promised each other "always" become strangers, adversaries or sometimes unexpected allies on the long road back to one another.

This book was born in those rooms.

Not from gossip, not from voyeurism and never from identifiable stories, but from themes, patterns, truths and the deeply human struggles I have witnessed time and time again.

Behind every chapter lies a familiar crossroads:

- the moment love falters
- the moment truth disrupts
- the moment pain speaks louder than affection
- the moment growth demands bravery

Couples rarely come to therapy because they have stopped loving one another.

More often, they come because they have forgotten how to love each other in the chaos of everyday life.

In these pages, you will find stories of betrayal, grief, rekindling, rediscovery, miscommunication, trauma, desire, resentment, repair and resilience. You will meet couples who broke apart, couples who rebuilt stronger than before and couples who realised that letting go was its own act of love.

No chapter is any one couple.

Every chapter is many couples.

My hope is that as you read, you will recognise pieces of your own relationship, not to frighten you, not to shame you, but to offer insight, compassion and perhaps a little courage.

If you are a couple reading this together, let it be a mirror that reflects both your wounds and your strengths.

If you are a therapist, may it serve as a companion to deepen the understanding you already hold.

And if you are someone quietly trying to understand why loving another human can be so astonishingly difficult, may these pages remind you that you are profoundly, beautifully, imperfectly human.

Love is not something we find.

It is something we learn, unlearn, practise and choose, often more than once.

Thank you for opening these stories.

Thank you for being brave enough to look within them.

Rachel Hilton

East Anglia, UK

Betrayal Between Messages

Anna sat down on the edge of the chair, her arms folded tightly across her chest. She did not look at David, who shifted awkwardly, his eyes fixed on the floor. The silence between them filled the room long before either spoke, heavy and tense, already grieving something that had not fully broken yet.

Anna finally inhaled sharply.

"He tells women online things he has never said to me. He calls them gorgeous, says he loves their smile, and sends them kisses at the end of every message. When was the last time he said anything like that to me?"

David rubbed the back of his neck.

"It is just banter. I have never met them. I never would. It is harmless."

Anna's eyes glistened.

"Harmless? You are telling other women you love them. You do not even say that to me anymore."

There had been no hotel rooms, no late-night disappearances, no physical betrayal. But the intimacy he had poured into strangers had drained the heart of their relationship.

In therapy, I asked David quietly:

"What do those conversations give you that your marriage does not right now?"

He hesitated.

"It is easy with them. They do not nag; they do not judge. They make me feel wanted. Anna used to… but now…"

Anna's tears spilt.

"I have been looking after the kids, paying the bills when you were out drinking, but somehow it is my fault you do not feel wanted?"

That was the moment David stopped defending and started seeing.

Weeks later, during a quieter session, Anna whispered:

"It is not that you said those things to them… it is that you stopped saying them to me."

And that became their turning point. The truth beneath the betrayal was not about other women at all. It was about neglect.

Lessons for Couples

- Emotional intimacy given elsewhere wounds as deeply as physical affairs.

- Dismissing your partner's pain as overreacting breaks trust further.
- Repair begins when accountability replaces justification.
- Small, daily expressions of affection protect relationships from drifting.

Lessons for Therapists

- Name emotional affairs clearly, without minimising or moralising.
- Help the betrayed partner articulate loss as well as anger.
- Explore the unmet needs that fuel online intimacy, without excusing behaviour.
- Guide couples toward honest dialogue before repair work begins.

Learning to Be Playful Again

Sarah and Tom walked in looking more like weary colleagues than partners, polite, efficient and quietly distant. Sarah's smile was courteous but tired, her eyes searching for something she could not quite name. Tom carried the heaviness of a man who had forgotten how to exhale. They sat side by side, not touching, their bodies angled forward as if bracing for another task to get through.

The atmosphere between them was muted and flat, two good people lost in routine.

No explosions, no betrayal, no crisis, just a slow fading of warmth.

Sarah sighed.

"We do not laugh anymore. We do not do silly things. Everything is serious."

Tom nodded, staring at his hands.

"I would not even know how to start. Play feels childish now."

Their life had become predictable. Work, school runs, bills, chores, sleep.

The problem was not a lack of love but a lack of lightness.

In therapy, we explored the small rituals they used to share: throwing cushions at each other, dancing in the kitchen, water fights with their kids, staying up late laughing at stupid TV shows. Somewhere along the way, adulthood had swallowed those moments whole.

I asked them to begin with tiny steps:

A board game.

A silly walk.

Cooking a meal together while playing their old playlist.

A shared joke, even if it felt forced at first.

The turning point came when Tom chuckled, a real, unscripted laugh, and said:

"I had forgotten what your laugh sounded like. I have missed it."

For Sarah, it felt like someone had reopened a window she did not realise had been closed.

For Tom, it was proof that joy had not died. It had just been neglected.

Together, they rekindled the small sparks that make love feel alive, not just functional.

Lessons for Couples

- Playfulness is not childish; it is bonding.
- Shared laughter restores closeness faster than difficult conversations alone.
- Small, silly rituals maintain warmth in long-term relationships.
- Intimacy grows when partners create joy, not just manage responsibilities.

Lessons for Therapists

- Normalise the loss of play in overstretched couples.
- Encourage micro-play, tiny manageable moments of fun.
- Explore barriers to play such as shame, fatigue or resentment.
- Reinforce that joy is a relational skill that can be relearned.

Menopause and Desire

Claire eased herself into the chair with the heaviness of someone carrying more than her years. Her blouse clung slightly at the neckline, a handkerchief twisting between her fingers. Jonathan sat opposite her, leaning forward, elbows on his knees, eyes soft but bewildered. Between them hung a mixture of tenderness and tension, two people mourning a closeness that once felt effortless.

Claire exhaled slowly.

"My body does not feel like mine anymore. I love Jonathan… but I do not want sex. And when I force myself, it hurts."

Jonathan's shoulders dropped.

"I feel shut out. She says it is menopause, but to me it feels like rejection."

Claire's voice trembled.

"I am not rejecting you. I am rejecting my own body. Everything has changed, and I hate that you think it is because of you."

Menopause had taken more than libido. It had taken Claire's confidence, her comfort in her own skin and her ability to feel relaxed in moments that once brought joy. Therapy became a place to talk openly about symptoms she felt embarrassed to name: dryness, fatigue, hot flushes, and the fear of being touched the wrong way.

Together, we explored new forms of intimacy: soft touch, longer moments of closeness, sensuality without expectation. Jonathan learned to slow down, to connect without pressure. Claire learned she did not need to perform; she needed to be honest.

The turning point came when Jonathan finally said quietly:

"I would rather adapt with you than lose you. I want closeness, not the version we used to have but the version we can create now."

For Claire, that lifted the weight of expectation.

For Jonathan, it gave him a new path forward: connection without fear.

Lessons for Couples

- Menopause changes intimacy but does not end it.
- New forms of closeness often deepen relationships.
- Empathy heals far more than pressure.
- Sexual connection should evolve with the body, not fight against it.

Lessons for Therapists

- Provide clear, shame-free psychoeducation on menopause.

- Encourage couples to redefine intimacy in broader, gentler ways.
- Normalise grief around changing bodies and shifting desire.
- Support partners in expressing needs without blame or fear.

Blended Beginnings

Samantha breezed in first, carrying the warm, welcoming energy of a woman used to making others feel comfortable. Her perfume lingered faintly of hairspray and citrus. Mark followed a step behind, shoulders squared, work boots heavy, the smell of fresh paint clinging to him. They sat close but not touching, two worlds joined by love yet divided by upbringing.

Samantha, a friendly and chatty hairdresser, had two children from a previous relationship, including twelve-year-old Jake, who was autistic. Mark, raised in a strict household after losing his mum young, had learned to man up early. Now, stepping into the role of stepdad brought unspoken tensions neither had language for.

Samantha sighed.

"When he criticises the kids, it feels like he is criticising me."

Mark shook his head.

"I am not criticising you. I just want them to learn respect. That is how I was raised. If I messed about, I got a clip round the ear. That is life."

The real clash was not parenting; it was childhoods meeting.

Samantha had been cherished.

Mark had been toughened.

Now their home was a collision of softness and structure.

Mark often labelled Jake lazy or rude, not understanding how autism shaped his behaviour. Samantha bristled at every comment, sensing threat rather than help.

The turning point came when Mark finally breathed out and said:

"I do not know how to deal with autism. I just do not understand it."

For Samantha, the confession softened everything.

For Mark, it opened the door to education instead of frustration.

What had been conflict became a shared learning journey rather than a battlefield.

Lessons for Couples

- Blending families requires patience, empathy and a willingness to learn from each other.
- Criticism of children often feels like criticism of parenting.
- Respect grows when partners choose understanding over assumption.
- Parenting differences often come from childhood wounds, not intention.

Lessons for Therapists

- Explore family-of-origin stories to reveal unspoken values.
- Offer psychoeducation when neurodiversity is misunderstood.
- Support couples in forming a united front rather than parallel systems.
- Encourage compassion for inherited parenting styles while guiding change.

"An affair of the heart can wound as deeply as one of the body."

The Emotional Affair

Lucy sat forward, her knuckles white around a crumpled tissue. Her lipstick was perfect, but her composure fragile. James leaned back with his arms folded, a half-smirk on his face that was more defence than defiance. The distance between them was not just physical; it was crowded with the presence of another woman, one who had never stepped into the room but had taken up space in their relationship all the same.

Lucy's voice trembled.

"He sends her good morning texts every day. When was the last time I got one? He ends his messages with kisses. He stopped doing that with me years ago."

James shrugged.

"It is not physical. She is just a mate. We talk. That is it."

But the truth was written across Lucy's face. This was not just talking.

James had quietly redirected his tenderness, the jokes, the soft moments, the intimate thoughts, away from his partner and towards someone else. The betrayal lived in the daily drip of attention that no longer belonged to Lucy.

The air between them thickened as Lucy whispered:

"It is not that he cheated. It is that he gave my place to her."

Therapy helped James confront something he had been avoiding: secrecy and emotional prioritising are forms of betrayal. He had convinced himself that because nothing physical had happened, nothing meaningful had happened either.

The turning point came when James finally said:

"I did not think it mattered if she got the best of me... and you only got what was left."

For Lucy, it was the first time her pain was acknowledged.

For James, it was the moment he stopped minimising and started understanding.

Lessons for Couples

- Emotional affairs can be as painful, or more painful, than physical ones.
- Withholding affection from one partner while giving it to another creates betrayal.
- Secrecy is often the real breach of trust.
- Repair begins with complete honesty and equal emotional availability.

Lessons for Therapists

- Name emotional infidelity clearly and without minimising.

- Validate the depth of hurt the betrayed partner experiences.
- Explore motivations behind the emotional shift without excusing it.
- Support the couple in redefining transparency, boundaries and emotional commitment.

When the Spark Fades

Emily sat with her shoulders slightly hunched, fingers tracing the hem of her sleeve as if trying to hold herself together. Peter stared at the carpet, jaw tight, his wedding ring catching the lamplight every time he shifted. The silence between them was not angry; it was hollow. Tired. The kind of silence that forms slowly over years of routine and unmet needs.

Emily's voice wavered.

"We do not laugh anymore. We barely touch. I feel like a ghost in my own marriage."

Peter exhaled heavily.

"I do not know what happened. Nothing is wrong, but nothing feels right either. I do not want us to end... I just do not know how to start again."

Their days revolved around work, children, chores and exhaustion. Nothing catastrophic had happened, and that almost made it worse. The relationship had simply drifted, like two boats tied loosely to the same harbour, no longer moving in sync.

In therapy, they explored what had been lost: playfulness, affection, curiosity, the tiny rituals that used to glue them together.

The turning point came when Peter finally admitted:

"I thought the spark would come back on its own. I did not realise we had to build it."

For Emily, that acknowledgement felt like a hand reaching through the fog.

For Peter, it was the first step toward seeing their marriage as alive, something that required tending, not waiting.

Lessons for Couples

- Sparks fade when connection is taken for granted, not because love disappears.
- Small, daily gestures rebuild intimacy more effectively than grand changes.
- Playfulness and curiosity need to be maintained, not left to memory.
- Emotional drift is reversible when both partners commit to reconnecting.

Lessons for Therapists

- Normalise relational flatness as a common stage, not a crisis.
- Help couples identify neglected rituals and sources of joy.
- Encourage structured reconnection practices: shared activities, touch, and presence.

- Explore emotional shutdown gently, without assigning blame.

"For some, pornography opens doors; for others, it builds walls. "

Pornography: Help or Hindrance?

Sophie entered first, confident but slightly tense, her laughter a little too light to be natural. Martin followed behind, shoulders rounded, eyes lowered, a man caught between shame and confusion. They sat close, yet the air between them felt thick with something private, something unspoken.

Sophie began slowly.

"Sometimes watching it together is fun. It adds something."

Martin swallowed.

"But I have been watching it alone. A lot. I hide it. And sometimes I would rather do that than… us."

For Sophie, pornography had been a shared spark.

For Martin, it had become a quiet escape.

The real issue was not pornography but secrecy, avoidance and the shame that kept him silent.

Weeks into therapy, Martin finally said, voice breaking:

"I did not realise how much it was replacing you."

That ownership softened Sophie's hurt and opened the door to rebuilding boundaries with honesty rather than secrecy.

Lessons for Couples

- Porn can enhance connection only when openly agreed upon.
- Secrecy damages trust more than viewing itself.
- Connection weakens when porn becomes a substitute for intimacy.
- Agreeing on boundaries together prevents silent resentment.

Lessons for Therapists

- Context matters; pornography is not inherently harmful.
- Explore shame and secrecy without judgement.
- Help couples negotiate boundaries explicitly.
- Support rebuilding trust through open conversations.

The Workplace Affair

Laura sat upright, arms folded, jaw clenched in quiet fury. Chris slumped beside her, eyes hollow, tie loosened like he had fought a battle he already knew he had lost. The tension between them was sharp, the scent of betrayal still fresh.

Laura spoke first.

"You used to talk to me that way. But now she gets your late-night texts. Your compliments. Your kisses."

Chris stared at the carpet.

"It started harmlessly. She listened. It felt easy."

Late-night messages blurred into lunches, then into hotel rooms. Chris insisted it meant nothing, but to Laura, the loss of emotional intimacy was the deepest cut.

Therapy forced honesty. No minimising. No shifting blame.

The turning point came when Chris finally said:

"I did not fall in love with her. I fell into feeling valued. But I broke us to feel it."

That admission allowed Laura to begin grieving what she lost, and deciding whether she still wanted what remained.

Lessons for Couples

- Workplace closeness can become intimacy without intention.
- Minimisation deepens pain; honesty creates the first crack of repair.
- Emotional affairs often wound more deeply than physical ones.
- Rebuilding requires clear boundaries around work and home.

Lessons for Therapists

- Name workplace affairs clearly; they are not harmless.
- Encourage full disclosure, not selective honesty.
- Support the betrayed partner's trauma response.
- Explore unmet emotional needs without excusing behaviour.

Secret Savings

Amira entered with trembling hands, her wedding ring catching the light, a symbol suddenly heavy with unspoken fear. Daniel sat stiffly beside her, arms folded, disbelief etched deeply across his face.

Amira spoke softly.

"I have been saving money… secretly. I was scared. Growing up, we always lost everything. I needed to feel safe."

Daniel's voice cracked.

"We are supposed to be a team. You let me believe we had nothing to hide."

Her secrecy was not malicious; it was survival.

His hurt was not about the money; it was about exclusion.

Therapy helped them uncover generational fears, poverty trauma and the instinct to hoard safety.

The turning point came when Amira whispered:

"I was not protecting the money. I was protecting the scared little girl I used to be."

Daniel finally understood her fear, and she finally understood his need for transparency.

Lessons for Couples

- Financial secrets wound trust as deeply as emotional betrayal.
- Hidden savings often stem from fear, not manipulation.
- Transparency builds safety for both partners.
- Couples must create shared financial rules to avoid secrecy.

Lessons for Therapists

- Explore the client's money story; childhood poverty shapes adult behaviour.
- Distinguish fear-driven secrecy from deliberate deception.
- Support couples in creating joint financial agreements.
- Normalise financial trauma and teach healthier coping strategies.

Menopause and Intimacy

Helen fanned herself lightly with a folded tissue, her cheeks flushed from more than nerves. She sat on the edge of the chair, shoulders drawn in as though even the air on her skin might sting. Mark leaned forward, hands clasped tightly, his face etched with worry and longing. Between them lay a mixture of ache, tenderness and confusion, two people wanting closeness but unsure how to find it again.

Helen exhaled.

"My body does not feel like mine anymore. The hot flushes, the dryness… sometimes it hurts just to be touched."

Mark swallowed hard.

"I thought you just did not want me. I thought I had lost you."

Helen shook her head, emotion tightening her throat.

"It is not you. It is my body. And I hate that you think it is rejection."

Menopause had shifted everything: her comfort, her confidence, her capacity for intimacy. Therapy became a place to slow the fear down, to educate them both about physical changes and to create a new language of closeness without pressure.

They explored gentler forms of intimacy: soft touch, connection without expectation, massage, and cuddling without the worry of where it would lead.

The turning point came when Mark finally said:

"I would rather adapt with you than live without you."

For Helen, those words let her breathe again. Intimacy could return without fear, without forcing and without shame.

Lessons for Couples

- Menopause changes intimacy, but closeness can evolve beautifully.
- Compassion eases fear; pressure deepens disconnection.
- New forms of touch can build a deeper connection.
- Understanding bodily changes reduces shame on both sides.

Lessons for Therapists

- Provide psychoeducation to reduce confusion and blame.
- Help couples redefine intimacy beyond intercourse.
- Normalise grief around changing bodies while offering hope.
- Encourage slow, safe conversations around comfort and boundaries.

*"Sometimes the hardest battles in a marriage are fought with
people who never step into the room."*

Blended Families and Adult Children

Janet walked in with the calm composure of a woman who had
defended herself one too many times. Her posture was proud, but
her eyes were tired. Paul followed close behind, shoulders heavy,
looking like a man stretched thin between loyalty and guilt. They sat
side by side but did not touch, united by marriage yet divided by the
pressure of family politics.

Both were in their late fifties, each bringing adult children into the
relationship. Janet had two grown children and an eight-year-old
still at home. Paul had three children in their thirties and forties, each
carrying unspoken fears about inheritance and loyalty.

Janet sighed.

"His children think I am after his money. I am not. I have worked
all my life. But they look at me like I am a gold-digger."

Paul rubbed his face.

"I have nearly lost her because of this. My kids do not see the
damage they are doing. Her children respect me. Why can't mine do
the same?"

The tension was not about money; it was grief, fear and identity
shifts. Paul's children saw Janet as a threat to the family they used
to have, and Janet constantly felt on trial.

The turning point came when Paul finally said:

"I cannot make my kids accept you. But I can make it clear that my marriage comes first."

For Janet, it was the first time she felt chosen rather than tolerated.

For Paul, it was the moment he stopped trying to placate everyone by sacrificing himself.

Lessons for Couples

- Adult children often project fear and loss onto new partners.
- Loyalty conflicts are normal, but must not define the marriage.
- A united front strengthens the relationship.
- Boundaries protect love; silence erodes it.

Lessons for Therapists

- Normalise resistance without excusing hostility.
- Explore grief, fear and identity shifts in adult children.
- Help couples create healthy family boundaries.
- Empower partners to prioritise their marriage openly.

The Quiet Withdrawal

Emma walked in with a polite smile stretched too tightly across her face, her hands folded neatly in her lap. David followed slowly, shoulders hunched, the look of someone who had forgotten how to exhale. They sat close enough to look like a couple, but the distance between them felt vast, the kind born not from fights but from silence.

Emma's voice wavered.

"He does not talk to me anymore. He answers me, but… it is like living with a shadow. He used to tell me everything."

David stared at the floor.

"I do not know what to say anymore. I feel like anything I say will be wrong. So I say nothing."

Their home was quiet, not peaceful but muted.

Emma felt invisible.

David felt like a failure.

The emotional withdrawal was slowly draining the relationship.

Emma whispered:

"I ask about his day… nothing. I tell him something funny… nothing. I cry, and he just sits there. I feel like I am disappearing."

David's voice cracked.

"It is not that I do not care. I am scared. When I am stressed, I shut down. I do not know how to be what she needs."

The turning point came when David finally looked at her properly and said:

"I did not realise my silence was hurting you. I thought I was protecting us from arguments. I did not know it made you feel alone."

For Emma, that truth softened years of hurt.

For David, it was the beginning of learning to stay present even when afraid.

Lessons for Couples

- Silence creates emotional distance as powerfully as conflict.
- Withdrawal is often fear, not indifference.
- Connection grows from small, consistent openness.
- Asking clearly for emotional needs prevents resentment from building.

Lessons for Therapists

- Explore each partner's conflict style gently.
- Normalise shutdown as a protective strategy while naming its impact.
- Teach emotional micro-connections that rebuild closeness.
- Reinforce safety so withdrawn partners risk vulnerability.

Spending Instead of Paying

Caroline entered slowly, eyes downcast, the faint scent of incense clinging to her clothes. She hugged her handbag tightly to her chest as though it could shield her from the consequences gathering around her. Matthew followed behind, shoulders heavy, his expression carved with disappointment. They sat apart, surrounded not by the things she had bought but by the security they had both lost.

Caroline's voice shook.

"I did not pay the bills. I bought things… crystals, candles, little ornaments. I could not stop."

Matthew swallowed hard.

"I thought the mortgage was covered. You let me believe we were safe."

Caroline twisted a tissue in her hands.

"I buried my head in the sand. I lied to myself before I lied to you."

Their home was days from repossession. What hurt Matthew was not the money; it was the deception, the quiet months of pretending everything was fine. Therapy uncovered the emotional truth: Caroline spent to soothe anxiety, to feel in control, to avoid the fear she could not name.

The turning point came when she whispered:

"I did not realise until it was too late that love cannot survive without honesty."

Caroline and Matthew ultimately separated, not out of anger but because the foundation they needed to rebuild was no longer there.

Lessons for Couples

- Financial secrecy erodes trust just as deeply as emotional betrayal.
- Compulsive spending often reflects unmet emotional needs.
- Facing financial reality together prevents long-term devastation.
- Repair is only possible with full transparency and accountability.

Lessons for Therapists

- Explore emotional drivers behind spending patterns.
- Assess financial communication early in therapy.
- Prepare couples for tough outcomes, including separation.
- Support clients in rebuilding self-esteem after financial mistakes.

Trauma Resurfacing

Natalie's hands trembled as she sat down, her breath shallow, eyes darting at every small sound. Martin sat beside her, knee bouncing, the picture of a man desperate to help but unsure how. The air between them was tense, not with anger but with fear: hers of the past, his of getting it wrong.

Natalie whispered:

"It is like my body remembers things I wish I could forget."

Martin reached for her hand; she flinched. Hurt flashed across his face.

"I am trying to help," he murmured.

"I know," she replied softly. "But when you get angry about it… I feel unsafe all over again."

Her trauma, buried for years, had resurfaced now that she finally felt safe. Quiet evenings and moments of intimacy triggered memories her body had never processed. Martin's instinct was rage at the abuser. Natalie needed gentleness, not a soldier preparing for war.

We explored grounding: noticing five things she could see, four she could touch, three she could hear. We also explored Martin's urge to rescue, intervening before it hardened into frustration.

The turning point came when Martin finally said:

"I thought being angry made me strong for you. But it only pushed you further away."

Natalie's tears fell.

"I did not need a fighter. I needed someone to sit with me in the dark."

That truth shifted their path from reaction to understanding, from fear to slow rebuilding.

Lessons for Couples

- Trauma often resurfaces when the body finally feels safe.
- Support means presence, not anger or rescuing.
- Healing requires patience, communication and choice.
- Intimacy must move at the survivor's pace.

Lessons for Therapists

- Work with both partners' nervous systems; trauma affects the whole relationship.
- Distinguish between protection and over-reaction.
- Use grounding techniques alongside talk therapy.
- Reframe resurfacing as a step toward healing, not a setback.

When She Hits Him

Liam walked in first, head lowered, shoulders rounded: a strong man carrying invisible bruises. Holly followed with a light laugh, tossing her hair, trying to soften the edges of something she did not want to name. They sat apart, the silence between them humming with discomfort.

Liam spoke quietly.

"She hits me. Slaps, sometimes punches. She says it does not hurt because I am bigger. But it does… here."

He placed a hand over his chest.

Holly scoffed lightly.

"He winds me up. He knows how to push my buttons. Look at him, he is huge. I could not hurt him even if I tried."

Liam's eyes filled.

"It is humiliating. I feel like less of a man. Who would believe me?"

Therapy exposed the truth: Holly's behaviour was not banter; it was not just temper; it was abuse. Minimisation had allowed her to justify it. Silence had forced Liam to endure it.

The turning point came when Liam finally cried, shoulders shaking, voice breaking. Holly froze, her expression shifting from defensiveness to shock.

Her voice softened.

"I did not realise I had broken you."

It was the first honest moment they had shared in years.

Lessons for Couples

- Abuse is abuse, regardless of gender or size.
- Minimising harm deepens injury and delays change.
- Accountability is necessary for repair.
- Emotional safety must come before rebuilding intimacy.

Lessons for Therapists

- Challenge cultural stereotypes that silence male victims.
- Hold the abusive partner accountable without shaming them into collapse.
- Develop safety plans for both partners.
- Support survivors in rebuilding boundaries and self-worth.

Holding On to Every Mistake

Claire sat perfectly upright, her hands clasped tightly in her lap, every movement precise as though even her posture might be judged. Adam leaned back, exhaling through his nose, the look of a man exhausted by apologies that never seemed to expire. The tension between them was not fiery; it was slow erosion, the damage that comes from years of keeping score.

Claire admitted quietly:

"My dad was away with the military for months. My mum kept a notebook of everything we did wrong so he could punish us when he got back. I think… I am still keeping that book in my head."

Adam sighed.

"She remembers things I said years ago. I cannot live anything down. And if I mention her mistakes, she gets hurt. I feel like I am always on trial."

Therapy gently unravelled how Claire had learned that mistakes were not moments, they were offences filed away for later. Her childhood had taught her to hold on, not to repair.

The turning point came when Claire whispered:

"I do not want to be my mum, keeping score. I do not want to keep punishing us."

For both, it was the first moment of hope, the realisation that forgiveness is a choice, not a weakness.

Lessons for Couples

- Keeping score poisons the connection and trust.
- Forgiveness is an active choice that frees both partners.
- Letting go requires unlearning childhood conditioning.
- Repair happens when partners talk about hurt instead of storing it.

Lessons for Therapists

- Explore family-of-origin patterns around blame and accountability.
- Model healthier forms of apology and repair.
- Help clients differentiate naming hurt from weaponising it.
- Reinforce that closure comes from processing, not storing grievances.

In-Laws, Boundaries and Power Struggles

Naomi sat forward, frustration radiating from every gesture, her voice already tight before she spoke. James leaned back, arms crossed, the posture of a man torn between loyalty to the woman who raised him and the woman he chose. The air held the familiar heaviness of too many phone calls, too many criticisms and too many silent car rides home.

Naomi groaned:

"His mother calls every day. Every day. She criticises my cooking, my job, and even how I dress. And he just sits there. He says nothing."

James looked down.

"My mum… she has always been like that. I do not want to upset her."

Naomi's voice cracked.

"And you do not mind upsetting me?"

Therapy revealed a lifelong pattern: James had been trained to keep the peace at home by staying quiet. Silence was his survival strategy, but in marriage, it became a weapon he did not intend to use.

The turning point came when James finally said:

"I am scared of disappointing her. But I am more scared of losing you."

For the first time, Naomi felt chosen.

For James, it was the moment he learned that boundaries are not disloyalty; they are protection.

Lessons for Couples

- Boundaries protect the relationship, not attack the family.
- Silence often communicates complicity more than neutrality.
- Loyalty must be shared, not split between partner and parent.
- Change begins when both partners stand together as a united front.

Lessons for Therapists

- Normalise the guilt partners feel when setting boundaries.
- Explore family conditioning around obedience, conflict and approval.
- Support couples in creating agreed-upon scripts for difficult interactions.

- Emphasise the importance of prioritising the marital unit.

Family Rejection Vs. Acceptance

Elliot and Marcus entered hand in hand, though Marcus let go the moment they sat down. Elliot's warmth filled the room, the ease of someone who had always been accepted. Marcus's posture was stiffer, guarded, the posture of someone who had learned to brace for impact.

Elliot smiled sadly.

"My family loves him. They treat him like one of us. Sunday dinners, birthdays, holidays… he is included."

Marcus looked away.

"My family still pretends I am straight. They do not acknowledge Elliot. He is invisible."

The contrast was painful. One family embraced. The other was erased.

Elliot squeezed Marcus's hand.

"I do not need your family to adore me. I just need them to see me."

Marcus whispered:

"They do not even say your name."

Therapy explored how this rejection seeped into their relationship: Marcus's shame, Elliot's loneliness and the unfairness of one partner always being the strong one.

The turning point came when Marcus said:

"I cannot change them. But I can change what I allow. If they cannot accept us, then they do not get access to us."

For Elliot, it was the first time Marcus put their relationship above his fear.

For Marcus, it was an act of courage years in the making.

Lessons for Couples

- Unequal family acceptance creates hidden power imbalances.
- Boundaries protect partners from emotional harm.
- Validation from each other matters more than external approval.
- Couples must decide together what behaviour they will tolerate from families.

Lessons for Therapists

- Explore internalised shame and the impact of unequal family support.
- Help couples develop united boundaries around family engagement.
- Normalise grief when families reject a partner's identity.

- Encourage relationship-centred decision-making over guilt-based obligations.

Emotional Overload and Sibling Rivalries

David walked in looking drained, dark circles shadowing his eyes, his phone buzzing silently with calls he could not bear to answer. Anna followed quietly, arms folded, shoulders tense, the posture of someone who had held it all together for far too long. They sat side by side, close but disconnected, the weight of family obligation pressing harder than either could carry alone.

David rubbed the bridge of his nose.

"My brothers never lift a finger for Mum. It is always me. Every appointment, every crisis. And it is killing my marriage."

Anna nodded, her voice taut.

"He will not say no. He runs himself into the ground, and we are the ones who pay for it. He is exhausted. I am exhausted. And his family do not even see it."

David sighed.

"If I do not do it, nobody will. She needs me."

Therapy revealed a lifetime of patterns: David as the responsible one, the good son, the fixer. His brothers had learned to step back because he always stepped forward. Anna was not fighting his loyalty; she was fighting the consequences.

The turning point came when Anna said softly:

"I am not asking you to abandon your mum. I am asking you not to abandon us."

For the first time, David saw that rescuing his family of origin was costing him his family of choice.

Lessons for Couples

- When one partner carries all caregiving, resentment grows silently.
- Healthy boundaries honour the parent without sacrificing the marriage.
- Saying no can be an act of love, not rejection.
- Shared caregiving decisions strengthen teamwork.

Lessons for Therapists

- Map out family-of-origin roles to uncover entrenched patterns.
- Help couples balance loyalty to parents with loyalty to each other.
- Promote practical, realistic boundaries rather than idealistic ones.
- Encourage joint planning instead of reactive crisis responses.

The Social Media Obsession

Hannah arrived immaculate, every strand of hair in place, her phone already propped for a quick behind-the-scenes clip before the session even began. Paul followed behind, hands in pockets, looking like a man who had long stopped trying to compete with the camera. They sat close, but her attention flicked constantly toward her screen, a third presence neither could silence.

Hannah flicked her hair.

"I plan my life around TikTok trends. The house, the holidays, and even how the kids dress. I just want it all to look perfect."

Paul shook his head.

"I do not care about matching sofas or Instagram kitchens. I care about us. But it feels like she would rather film our life than live it."

Hannah insisted:

"It inspires me. It motivates me to be better."

Paul's voice softened.

"But it makes me feel like I will never be enough."

Therapy helped Hannah explore the craving beneath the content: validation, affirmation and escape. The pressure to perform had replaced genuine connection.

The turning point came when Hannah finally whispered:

"Sometimes… I forget I have a life offline."

Lessons for Couples

- Social media can inspire, but it can also create relentless pressure.
- Offline connection must matter more than online perception.
- Honest conversations about validation restore balance.
- Couples thrive when they agree on tech boundaries together.

Lessons for Therapists

- Explore themes of self-worth and external validation.
- Help couples negotiate realistic boundaries around phones and posting.
- Highlight the difference between aspiration and comparison.
- Encourage mindfulness around the emotional impact of social media.

Living in a Shadow

Laura sat with her hands folded tightly in her lap, the silver locket around her neck catching the light, a constant reminder of the man she had lost. Michael leaned back, posture rigid but eyes weary, the look of someone who had been living beside a memory instead of a wife. Between them lay thick silence, filled with love, guilt and the ghost neither could escape.

Laura spoke first.

"My first marriage was rocky. We were talking about divorce when he died. But now… I only remember the good bits. I compare Michael to him, and it is not fair."

Michael looked down.

"I cannot compete with a ghost. It feels like he is in our bed every night."

Therapy revealed Laura's grief, guilt and the subtle romanticising that follows a tragic ending. Death had frozen her first husband in amber: perfect, untouchable, impossible to measure up to.

The turning point came when Laura said:

"I need to grieve him honestly, not the man I wish he were."

It was the first time she allowed truth to soften the memory, making space for Michael to exist beside it.

Lessons for Couples

- Grief often idealises past partners, creating impossible comparisons.
- Current partners need room to be valued for who they are.
- Honest grieving restores emotional balance.
- Love cannot flourish while living in someone else's shadow.

Lessons for Therapists

- Normalise idealisation of deceased partners without endorsing it.
- Encourage balanced remembering: both the good and the difficult.
- Help couples separate grief work from relationship work.
- Support the present partner in expressing needs without guilt.

Old Trauma, New Relationship

Sophie sat curled into herself, eyes fixed on the floor, her hands clasped so tightly her knuckles whitened. Ben sat beside her, fists clenched, jaw tight, the image of a man built for battle but fighting the wrong war. The silence between them carried the weight of history: pain neither of them had caused, but both were now forced to live with.

Sophie had been sexually abused in her teens. Years later, with partner Ben, the echoes remained.

She spoke quietly.

"When he touches me a certain way, I panic. He thinks it is about him. It is not."

Ben's voice wavered between anger and helplessness.

"I want to protect her. But I also want to hurt the man who did this. I hate that he is still in our bed."

Sophie did not need revenge; she needed safety. Therapy helped Ben understand that Sophie's trauma lived in her nervous system, not in her intentions. His instinct to fight made her body tense even more.

The turning point came when Ben finally said:

"I cannot fight your past. But I can stand beside you in the present."

For Sophie, that shifted everything.

For Ben, it transformed him from rescuer to partner.

Lessons for Couples

- Past trauma often intrudes on present intimacy.
- Partners must resist the urge to retaliate against ghosts.
- Healing comes through patience, calm and emotional safety.
- Intimacy must move at the survivor's pace, not the partner's urgency.

Lessons for Therapists

- Validate the partner's anger while redirecting it constructively.
- Focus on nervous-system safety, not rapid trauma repair.
- Teach grounding and trauma-informed intimacy.
- Normalise setbacks as part of the healing arc.

Married Too Young

Abbie sat small in her chair, twisting her wedding ring round and round, the metal glinting under the light like a reminder of promises made too soon. Daniel leaned back, shoulders slumped, eyes tired but kind. They looked more like childhood friends than lovers, two people bound by history rather than passion.

They had married at seventeen after an unexpected pregnancy. Fifteen years and three children later, they found themselves in therapy searching for truth rather than rescue.

Abbie spoke first.

"We have never known life outside of each other. But now, I do not even know who I am."

Daniel nodded slowly.

"I love her. But I feel like we have grown into different people."

Seven sessions explored their shared history: routines, responsibilities and the way they had aged into roles rather than choices. They tried to find a bridge, but the foundation had been built on necessity, not compatibility.

The turning point was gentle and heartbreaking: both admitting that staying together out of duty was hurting them more than separating.

Abbie whispered:

"Maybe the bravest thing we can do is let go."

And Daniel, with tears in his eyes, agreed.

Lessons for Couples

- Early marriages often leave little space for individual growth.
- Love can remain even when a partnership cannot.
- Separation can be an act of respect, not failure.
- Honest endings protect children more than forced togetherness.

Lessons for Therapists

- Honour the love that still exists, even in endings.
- Support couples in separating without blame.
- Help partners grieve the relationship while celebrating growth.
- Frame transitions as paths to authenticity rather than collapse.

The Hidden Child

Olivia sat rigid, eyes red but defiant, the tissue in her hand shredded into tiny pieces. Jack's head hung low, his voice quiet, the tone of a man who had run out of excuses. Between them lay years of trust suddenly cracked open by a truth that could not be undone.

Olivia's voice trembled.

"You had a child before we met… and you never told me."

Jack swallowed hard.

"I thought it would ruin everything. I thought if I kept quiet long enough, it would disappear."

But secrets do not disappear; they grow roots.

Jack had fathered a child in his early twenties. Shame, denial and fear kept him silent through the first dates, the engagement, the wedding and the birth of their own children. The truth surfaced only when the teenager reached out wanting to know his father.

Olivia was not just grieving the lie; she was grieving the version of their marriage she thought she had.

The turning point came when Jack said softly:

"I did not hide him because I did not care. I hid him because I was scared you would leave. But by hiding it, I made the thing I feared most happen anyway."

For Olivia, the wound was deep. But truth, finally spoken, became the first step toward deciding what came next with clarity rather than illusion.

Lessons for Couples

- Secrets create distance long before they surface.
- Hidden children represent hidden selves: grief, shame and fear.
- Repair requires transparency, not justification.
- Trust can only be rebuilt if both partners commit to full honesty moving forward.

Lessons for Therapists

- Explore emotional drivers behind long-term secrecy.
- Support both partners through shock, grief and identity rupture.
- Help couples rebuild through structured, gradual transparency.
- Validate the complexity: love can survive secrets, but not silence.

Falling in Love After Sixty

George and Alan entered with the quiet warmth of two men who had already lived whole lives, finally allowing themselves to live truthfully. George's hands fidgeted with the cuff of his jumper, betraying nerves beneath his gentle smile. Alan sat close, confident yet tender, his knee brushing George's in reassurance.

They were both in their sixties, discovering a kind of love they had each been denied for decades.

George said softly:

"I feel like a teenager. And also like a fraud. I do not know how to do this openly."

Alan nodded.

"I have spent my life hiding, too. But I do not want to hide anymore."

Their families varied in support. One son welcomed the relationship wholeheartedly; a daughter refused to speak about it. Therapy helped them navigate the joy of rediscovering love and the grief of relationships strained by their truth.

The turning point came when George whispered:

"I have spent so long living small. I do not want fear to steal this, too."

Alan took his hand.

"It will not. Not this time."

Together, they began building a love that did not need to apologise for existing.

Lessons for Couples

- Later-life love brings both freedom and old fears.
- Authenticity can strain relationships but strengthen identity.
- Joy is allowed at any age.
- Healing past suppression often strengthens present love.

Lessons for Therapists

- Validate the grief of years lived in hiding.
- Explore intergenerational reactions with compassion.
- Support clients in building pride, not just tolerance.
- Honour the importance of chosen family alongside biological family.

A Secret Affair with A Friend's Partner

Isla entered pale, eyes swollen, every movement tentative as though afraid the air itself might shatter. Luke followed a step behind, jaw tight, his silence louder than shouting. They sat apart, both staring at the floor. Not just a relationship had broken; a whole friendship circle had cracked with it.

Isla swallowed hard.

"I never meant for it to happen. He is my best friend's partner. It started with jokes, late-night chats… and then one night it crossed a line."

Luke's voice shook.

"You betrayed me with someone who sits at our table. How do I face any of them again?"

The affair had torn through two relationships and an entire group dynamic. Therapy navigated the grief of multiple losses: trust, belonging, safety and identity within their social world.

Isla finally admitted:

"It was not just about him. It was about feeling wanted. And I forgot what it would cost."

The turning point came when Luke said quietly:

"You did not just cheat on me. You cheated on our whole world."

Some wounds heal; some simply become truth. Their work became less about repair and more about deciding whether anything worth saving remained.

Lessons for Couples

- Affairs with friends' partners cause wide-reaching relational damage.
- Betrayal ripples beyond the couple into social circles.
- Repair requires radical honesty or the courage to end.
- Both partners must grieve the social fallout, not just the affair.

Lessons for Therapists

- Explore the relational ecosystem, not just the romance.
- Validate the betrayed partner's social losses.
- Address identity crises triggered by community fractures.
- Guide clients in rebuilding connections or creating new ones.

When One Partner Checks Out

Ella entered first, shoulders slumped, her coat still half-on as though she was not sure she wanted to stay. Tom followed slowly, hands buried in his pockets, eyes fixed on the carpet. They sat side by side but angled away from each other, two people who looked more like flatmates who shared bills than lovers who once shared dreams.

Ella spoke quietly:

"It feels like he is not here anymore. He eats with me, sleeps next to me… but I cannot feel him."

Tom shrugged.

"I do not know what to say. Work has been hard. I am tired."

But the truth ran deeper. Tom had not cheated, had not argued, had not stormed out or threatened to leave. He had simply faded.

Conversations were short. Touch had stopped. Plans were maybe later.

Ella felt unwanted; Tom felt overwhelmed.

Ella wiped her eyes.

"I would rather have an argument than this silence. At least an argument means you care."

Therapy revealed Tom's coping style: shutting down to avoid burdening anyone. Ella interpreted the withdrawal as rejection; he believed withdrawal was protection.

The turning point came when Tom whispered, barely audible:

"I did not step back because I stopped loving you. I stepped back because I did not know how to show up when I felt empty."

For the first time, they were not fighting each other; they were fighting the silence together.

Lessons for Couples

- Emotional withdrawal is as damaging as conflict, often more.
- Naming overwhelm reduces fear of abandonment.
- Connection requires small, daily bids for closeness, not perfection.
- Repair begins when both partners face the silence instead of avoiding it.

Lessons for Therapists

- Identify avoidant coping styles early; they often masquerade as calm.
- Help couples translate silence into emotion and unmet needs.
- Support rebuilding micro-connections: touch, check-ins, shared routines.

- Validate the withdrawing partner's overwhelm without excusing behaviour.

Weight, Shame and Desire

Chloe sat with her arms folded tightly across her chest, as if shielding herself from her own body. Her eyes glistened but never lifted to meet Nathan's. Nathan leaned forward, elbows on his knees, his voice gentle but edged with helplessness. The air between them was thick with unspoken apologies: Chloe for hiding, Nathan for not knowing how to help her see what he still saw, the woman he loved.

Chloe whispered:

"I do not want you to see me. Not like this. I feel disgusting."

Nathan shook his head slowly.

"You have changed… but not in the way you think. I still want you. I miss you. I miss us."

Chloe's shame ran deep, rooted in old comments from family, pregnancies and the quiet erosion of confidence over the years. She avoided intimacy, convinced Nathan's desire had evaporated as her weight changed.

Nathan finally admitted:

"It is not your body that is shutting me out. It is you."

Therapy helped Chloe unpick where her shame began, and helped Nathan realise that reassurance alone could not undo years of internalised judgement.

The turning point came when Chloe said:

"I do not want to disappear from my own life anymore."

It was not about weight; it was about worth.

Lessons for Couples

- Desire fades faster from shame than from physical change.
- Openness about insecurity creates more intimacy than avoidance.
- Attraction is multidimensional; emotional closeness fuels physical closeness.
- Patience and compassion rebuild confidence more effectively than reassurance alone.

Lessons for Therapists

- Explore the historical roots of body shame, not just present conflict.
- Help partners separate personal insecurity from relational dynamics.
- Encourage gradual, consent-based reconnection to intimacy.

- Normalise grief around changing bodies while promoting self-compassion.

Messaging the Friend

Amelia sat rigid on the edge of the sofa, arms folded tightly across her chest. Josh slumped beside her, hands clasped, jaw tight, eyes refusing to meet hers. The silence in the room felt brittle, the kind that has already said too much. Amelia's eyes were sore from crying; Josh looked trapped between defensiveness and shame.

Amelia's voice trembled.

"My friend told me everything. The good morning messages with kisses. The jokes. The late-night chats. All while you were lying next to me in bed."

Josh muttered:

"It was nothing. Just banter. Nothing happened."

Amelia's face hardened.

"Nothing? You gave her what you took away from me. You made me look jealous, paranoid, when I was not wrong at all."

This was not a physical affair, but an emotional one, fed quietly through secrecy and crossed boundaries. Therapy centred on transparency, understanding why Josh sought validation elsewhere and the painful truth that minimising only deepened the wound.

The turning point came when Josh finally said:

"I was not looking for her. I was looking for something I lost in myself… and it cost me you."

Lessons for Couples

- Emotional affairs erode trust as deeply as physical ones.
- Secrecy, not sex, is often the real betrayal.
- Rebuilding requires honesty, boundaries and consistency.
- Validation from others cannot fill the voids within the relationship.

Lessons for Therapists

- Validate emotional betrayal without minimising the harm.
- Explore unmet needs that led to secrecy.
- Support the betrayed partner through grief and anger.
- Guide couples toward clear, mutually agreed communication boundaries.

Flirting with His Friend

Sienna entered with sharp, confident energy, chin lifted, expression unreadable. Alex trailed behind her, shoulders heavy, moving with the weight of humiliation rather than anger. On the sofa, they sat at opposite ends: Sienna cross-legged and defensive, Alex leaning forward, staring at the floor as though trying to piece together where everything went wrong.

Sienna spoke first.

"It was just flirting. Emojis. Little jokes. Nothing happened."

Alex's voice cracked.

"He is my mate. You sent him things you never sent me. Do you know what that felt like?"

Sienna rolled her eyes, but her bravado was thinning.

"I did not think it meant anything."

But it had meant something, not to the friend but to her: the thrill, the attention, the feeling of being desired. She carried that energy home to Alex, never admitting where it came from.

Alex finally said:

"You did not cheat on me. You cheated on our trust."

Therapy unpacked the role of ego, boredom and unmet emotional needs. The turning point came when Sienna whispered:

"I liked how he made me feel… until I saw how it made you feel."

It was the first moment she stopped defending herself and started truly seeing him.

Lessons for Couples

- Flirting becomes harmful when it replaces connection at home.
- Secrecy is the first sign a boundary has been crossed.
- Repair requires empathy, not excuses.
- Couples must define their own limits around digital behaviour.

Lessons for Therapists

- Explore the emotional payoff of the flirtation without shaming.
- Clarify digital boundaries with both partners.
- Address self-esteem and attention-seeking patterns.
- Support repair through transparency and accountability.

Unequal Loads at Home

Emma looked exhausted in that quiet, contained way, hair scraped back, laptop bag still in hand, as though she had rushed straight from holding the world together. Tom followed behind, scrolling on his phone until she began speaking. They sat down with contrasting energy: Emma upright and tense, Tom leaning back as if the sofa might swallow him whole.

Emma spoke first.

"I earn more than double what he does. I work full-time. But I come home to chaos while he relaxes. I feel like I have two jobs."

Tom frowned.

"I do stuff! Just… not the way she wants. And I'm stressed too."

But Emma carried the emotional ledger of every undone task, every ignored responsibility, every moment she felt like a single mother in a marriage.

Therapy revealed the pattern: Emma over-functioned, Tom under-functioned. Neither felt appreciated; both felt misunderstood.

The turning point came when Tom finally said:

"I didn't realise you were drowning. I thought you were just… better at holding everything."

Emma's tears told the truth: she did not want to be better; she wanted to be partnered.

Lessons for Couples

- Fairness is about impact, not identical workloads.
- Emotional labour counts as real labour.
- Naming overwhelm is essential; resentment grows in silence.
- Repair requires shared responsibility, not score-keeping.

Lessons for Therapists

- Explore family models of labour and who taught each partner their role.
- Help couples build practical, realistic division-of-labour plans.
- Address resentment before behavioural change.
- Reinforce teamwork rather than blame.

Obsessed with the Ex

Anna's sadness seemed to arrive before she did, her shoulders sinking, eyes cast downward, voice small and tired. Ben entered mid-story, the kind of anxious chatter that fills silence he did not want to face. On the sofa, Anna folded inward; Ben sat forward, animated and defensive.

Anna whispered:

"He checks his ex-wife's Facebook every day. He talks about her constantly. I feel like I'm living with both of them."

Ben huffed.

"I just don't want to be made a fool of again. She lied to me. She hurt me. I'm just… keeping an eye on things."

But Anna felt the weight of being compared to a ghost, measured against a woman she did not even know.

Therapy helped Ben explore why he clung so tightly to the past. It was not love, it was fear, humiliation, and unfinished grief.

The turning point came when Ben admitted:

"I thought watching her would protect me. But it's only hurting you and us."

Anna nodded, finally feeling seen.

Lessons for Couples

- Constant monitoring of an ex traps the relationship in the past.
- Trust requires emotional presence, not surveillance.
- New partners need to feel chosen, not compared.
- Healing requires letting go of old wounds.

Lessons for Therapists

- Explore the grief beneath obsession, betrayal, shame, and loss.
- Highlight the impact of emotional triangulation.
- Encourage boundaries around digital monitoring.
- Support couples in building a forward-focused narrative.

Digital Voyeurism

Clara's anger was tightly coiled beneath her calm voice, jaw tense, eyes sharp enough to slice through the air. Liam sat beside her, shoulders hunched, hands fidgeting, guilt written across every movement. They did not look at each other. The room felt cold, the fallout of digital betrayal lingering like static.

Clara began:

"I found all the profiles. Women he follows. Comments he leaves. Messages. He says it's nothing, but it feels like something."

Liam swallowed hard.

"It's just looking. I've never met any of them. It's not cheating."

But Clara's pain was not about whether bodies touched. It was about secrecy, comparison, and the quiet erosion of trust.

"He compares me to strangers," she said. "I feel like I'm auditioning in my own marriage."

The turning point came when Liam murmured:

"I didn't realise my scrolling was making you feel replaced."

It was not the digital behaviour alone. It was the hiding, the shame, the secrecy.

Lessons for Couples

- Digital behaviour carries emotional impact even without physical contact.
- Transparency stops small cracks from becoming fractures.
- Comparison damages connection and self-worth.
- Repair begins with acknowledging the emotional betrayal.

Lessons for Therapists

- Normalise digital confusion; the rules are still evolving.
- Explore the difference between fantasy and harm.
- Address shame without excusing secrecy.
- Help couples build shared digital boundaries and agreements.

Love After Sixty

Patricia and Edward arrived already holding hands, not tightly, but with a gentle reassurance that spoke of second chances. Patricia radiated warmth and quiet confidence, the energy of a woman who had lived, learned, and refused to repeat old mistakes. Edward looked slightly bemused but hopeful, the cautious optimism of a man unused to this level of emotional honesty.

They sat close on the sofa, bodies angled naturally towards each other, laughter never far from the surface. There was a softness in the room, two people unlearning old patterns, rebuilding trust at an age where many give up trying.

Patricia smiled gently.

"I want to do this with open eyes. I don't want to fall into old habits."

Edward nodded, fiddling with his sleeve.

"I've never talked this openly in a relationship. But I want to get it right this time."

Their work focused on communication styles shaped by previous marriages, his avoidance, and her over-responsibility. The turning point came when Edward admitted:

"I realised I listened to you the way I wish my first wife had listened to me, but I never actually showed you how to love me back."

For Patricia, that honesty was the beginning of trust.

Lessons for Couples

- Love later in life requires unlearning old patterns.
- Emotional honesty accelerates connection.
- Second chances deserve clarity, not assumptions.
- Tenderness deepens when both partners bring self-awareness.

Lessons for Therapists

- Explore past relationship templates with curiosity.
- Support clients in naming needs without shame.
- Encourage vulnerability as an intentional skill.
- Highlight the importance of pacing and emotional safety.

Learning to Be Playful Again

When they walked in, they looked more like weary colleagues than partners, polite, efficient, quietly distant. Sarah's smile was thin, her eyes tired. Tom carried the heaviness of a man who had forgotten how to exhale. They sat side by side, bodies angled forward as though bracing for another task.

Their relationship had become serious, functional, flat.

Sarah spoke quietly.

"We don't laugh anymore. Everything is chores or work."

Tom nodded.

"I wouldn't even know where to start. Play feels… childish."

Their sessions focused on reintroducing small sparks, not grand gestures, but tiny interactions. A board game. A water fight with the kids. A shared playlist in the kitchen. Slowly, joy returned in flickers.

The turning point came when Tom chuckled during a session and said:

"I forgot what your laugh sounded like. I've missed it."

For Sarah, that moment was worth more than any romantic gesture.

For Tom, it was proof that lightness could coexist with responsibility.

Lessons for Couples

- Playfulness is not childish, it is connective.
- Shared joy rebuilds emotional intimacy.
- Seriousness alone cannot sustain a relationship.
- Laughter softens old resentments.

Lessons for Therapists

- Encourage small, frequent playful rituals.
- Highlight the role of shared joy in attachment.
- Normalise couples forgetting how to have fun.
- Explore resistance to play as fear or vulnerability.

Secret Savings

When they arrived, Mark's hurt was written across his face, eyes red, jaw tight, the look of someone whose foundation had been quietly shaken. Lucy sat beside him, composed but guarded, hands clasped tightly in her lap as though holding herself together.

Lucy had been siphoning money into a separate account for years. Mark discovered it by accident.

Mark's voice shook.

"All these years, I thought we were a team. Why didn't you tell me?"

Lucy stared at the floor.

"I needed to feel secure. I didn't grow up with much... having that account made me feel safe."

It was not the money that broke him; it was the secrecy.

Therapy explored Lucy's childhood fears and Mark's sense of betrayal. They learned to talk about finances without shame or defence. The turning point came when Lucy finally admitted:

"I wasn't saving money. I was saving myself... from a fear I never explained."

For Mark, understanding her fear softened the betrayal.

For Lucy, speaking it aloud dissolved years of secrecy.

Lessons for Couples

- Financial secrecy erodes trust even when intentions are not malicious.
- Money fears often stem from childhood experiences.
- Joint transparency builds emotional and financial safety.
- Repair requires empathy, not interrogation.

Lessons for Therapists

- Explore money narratives from the family of origin.
- Distinguish between secrecy, self-protection, and survival habits.
- Encourage open financial planning.
- Validate both fear (the saver) and betrayal (the partner).

The Ex Back in the Picture

Sophie entered with her arms crossed tightly, chin lifted in defiance; she did not quite feel. Liam followed behind, shoulders stiff, anger simmering in the space between them. They sat at opposite ends of the sofa, the emotional distance loud and overwhelming.

Sophie's ex had resurfaced online, liking old photos, sending casual messages, checking in "just to see how she was." What began as harmless nostalgia quickly became frequent chats she did not mention to Liam.

Liam's jaw clenched as he said:

"Every time he contacts you, you light up. Don't tell me it's just friendship. I feel like I'm competing with a ghost from your past."

Sophie whispered:

"I didn't tell you because I didn't want drama. He reminds me of who I used to be… not who I want now."

The turning point came when Liam added softly:

"I'm not afraid of him. I'm afraid of losing you."

For Sophie, the fear in his voice made her confront what she had been avoiding.

For both, transparency became the only way forward.

Lessons for Couples

- Old flames reignite insecurities that must be addressed openly.
- Secrets about communication create more damage than the contact itself.
- Emotional safety requires honesty, even when uncomfortable.
- Boundaries with ex-partners must be co-created, not assumed.

Lessons for Therapists

- Explore what the ex symbolises: identity, nostalgia, or unmet needs.
- Validate jealousy without letting it dominate.
- Support partners in creating realistic, shared boundaries.
- Highlight avoidance patterns that maintain secrecy.

The Affair Next Door

Hannah walked in pale and hollow-eyed, the kind of exhaustion that sleep could not touch. David followed, anger coiled tightly beneath the surface. They sat separately, both flinching at the sound of footsteps outside the window.

David had been unfaithful, not with a stranger but with their neighbour.

Every glance out of the kitchen window, every laugh drifting from next door, sharpened the wound.

Hannah whispered:

"I can't breathe in my own garden anymore."

David looked ashamed.

"It wasn't love, it was stupidity. I ended it. I'm here. But I can't undo it."

The turning point came when Hannah said:

"Then why does it still live next door?"

Therapy shifted from blame to survival, rearranging rooms, reclaiming spaces, establishing boundaries, and helping Hannah rebuild a sense of safety in the one place she should never have lost it.

Lessons for Couples

- Affairs with neighbours intensify trauma due to constant proximity.
- Emotional recovery requires reclaiming home as a safe space.
- Moving, distancing, or restructuring boundaries is often essential.
- Transparency and patience must be unwavering.

Lessons for Therapists

- Treat proximity-based betrayal as a complex trauma trigger.
- Support clients in environmental safety planning.
- Help partners navigate ongoing exposure without retraumatisation.
- Address guilt, shame, and the partner's need for secure space.

Religious Differences

Aisha entered with quiet grace, her eyes filled with conviction and sadness. Michael followed, looking worn down, as though caught between two worlds. They sat close, but their hands rested separately on their knees, each carrying the weight of generations behind them.

They had fallen in love effortlessly, but raising children exposed the cracks.

Aisha's faith was the core of her identity.

Michael feared religious pressure and wanted their children to choose freely.

Aisha said softly:

"My faith is my foundation. I want our children raised with it."

Michael replied:

"I don't want them to feel forced. Faith should be chosen, not inherited."

Their conflict was not really about religion; it was about fear of losing themselves or their children to a world the other did not fully understand.

The turning point came when Aisha whispered:

"I'm not trying to convert you. I just don't want to erase myself."

And Michael answered:

"And I don't want to disappear either."

Only then could they begin building a shared path.

Lessons for Couples

- Faith conflicts often mask deeper fears about identity and belonging.
- Children become symbolic battlegrounds unless couples communicate openly.
- Mutual respect matters more than agreement.
- Compromise requires creativity, not surrender.

Lessons for Therapists

- Attend to cultural and spiritual identities with sensitivity.
- Explore what each partner fears losing.
- Encourage collaborative parenting plans around values.
- Remain neutral and avoid reinforcing either worldview.

Love Across Colour Lines

Emily and James entered hand in hand, but the fatigue in Emily's eyes told another story. James's shoulders were tense, his voice quiet, the calm of a man used to keeping peace in rooms where he was not welcome.

Their relationship was solid.

Their families were not.

Emily said tearfully:

"My parents see his skin before they see him. They make comments… subtle, but sharp."

James nodded.

"And my family says she'll never understand what it's like for me. They smile at her face and question her heart behind closed doors."

The relationship itself was not the problem; the world around it was.

The turning point came when Emily whispered:

"We're fighting battles neither of us created."

And James replied:

"Then let's stop fighting each other and start fighting together."

Lessons for Couples

- Interracial relationships often face external pressures that exhaust the couple.
- Unity strengthens bonds against outside prejudice.
- Communication must include discussions of identity and lived experience.
- Boundaries with families may need to be firm and unapologetic.

Lessons for Therapists

- Validate the impact of racism and microaggressions on the relationship.
- Encourage the couple to share experiences of discrimination safely.
- Avoid colour-blind narratives; they invalidate lived reality.
- Promote collaborative coping strategies.

"Secrets don't stay small; they grow in the dark."

The Secret Fetish

Matt looked pale, almost translucent with anxiety, his hands trembling slightly as he took his seat. Claire sat beside him, arms folded, her expression a mixture of hurt, confusion, and anger. The air between them was fragile; one wrong word, and the whole thing might crack open again.

Claire spoke first.

"I found the drawer. The lingerie. The hidden things. I felt sick. Not because of what it was… but because you hid it."

Matt's voice wavered.

"I was terrified you'd think I was disgusting. I thought you'd leave."

For Claire, it was not the fetish, it was the secrecy. She felt shut out of a part of his identity he had been living alone. Therapy explored shame, expression, consent, and what it meant to bring hidden parts of oneself into a shared relationship.

The turning point came when Claire whispered:

"It's not the fetish that broke my trust. It's that you didn't trust me with it."

For Matt, that was the moment he realised healing meant honesty, not hiding.

Lessons for Couples

- Secrecy damages intimacy more deeply than sexual preference ever could.
- Vulnerability strengthens the connection when both partners stay curious rather than judgemental.
- Fantasies need conversation, consent, and shared boundaries.
- Trust is rebuilt through transparency, not silence.

Lessons for Therapists

- Normalise sexual diversity to reduce client shame.
- Separate secrecy from sexual identity in the therapeutic narrative.
- Support couples in negotiating boundaries around exploration.
- Help partners express fears without collapsing into judgement.

Living in a Saint's Shadow

Laura sat with her hands folded tightly in her lap, the silver locket around her neck catching the light—a reminder of the man she had lost. Paul sat beside her, polite but distant, as though part of him still lived beside the memory of his late wife.

They were not competing with another woman; they were competing with a ghost.

Laura exhaled shakily.

"I feel like I'm up against a version of her that never existed. You say she was perfect… but you told me yourself the marriage was broken."

Paul rubbed his forehead.

"I didn't mean to turn her into a saint. After she died… the guilt twisted everything."

Therapy helped them untangle grief from idealisation. Laura did not need Paul to stop loving his late wife—she needed room to exist beside the memory.

The turning point came when Laura whispered:

"I don't want to replace her. I just want to stop competing with her."

Paul finally nodded.

"You're not in her shadow. I'm just learning how to let the past be the past."

Lessons for Couples

- Grief can distort memories and idealise the past.
- New partners need space to be valued for who they are.
- Acknowledging the complexity of past relationships is essential for healing.
- Love can grow again when guilt loosens its grip.

Lessons for Therapists

- Normalise idealisation during grief processing.
- Encourage honest, balanced remembering.
- Help the new partner express their pain without shame.
- Support clients in integrating past and present love.

Messaging the Friend

Jason entered with confident swagger, leaning back in his chair as though expecting to charm his way through the session. Amy sat rigid beside him, her face pale with fury barely held together.

Amy finally said:

"You were sending her good morning texts. With kisses. Every single day. While I was lying next to you."

Jason rolled his eyes.

"It was just banter. Nothing happened."

But Amy's voice cracked.

"You told her not to tell me. That makes it something."

The betrayal was not physical—it was emotional, secretive, and humiliating. Therapy confronted Jason's minimisation, helping him understand that the issue was not flirting; it was the intimacy he had taken away from Amy and given to her friend.

The turning point came when Amy whispered:

"You gave her what you stopped giving me."

Jason finally saw the real wound—the absence, not the affair.

Lessons for Couples

- Emotional betrayal cuts as deeply as physical betrayal.
- Minimising a partner's pain worsens the rupture.
- Openness and accountability are non-negotiable for repair.
- Rebuilding trust requires consistent change, not promises.

Lessons for Therapists

- Name emotional affairs directly.
- Address minimisation and defensiveness early.
- Validate the betrayed partner's emotional experience.
- Facilitate structured honesty practices to rebuild trust.

The Hidden Child

Olivia sat rigidly, eyes red but defiant, a shredded tissue clutched in her hand. Jack's head hung low, voice quiet, the tone of a man who had run out of excuses.

Olivia spoke first.

"You let me build a life with you without telling me you had a child. A whole child. A whole human being."

Jack swallowed hard.

"I was ashamed. I didn't want you to leave. I thought I was protecting us."

But Olivia shook her head.

"You weren't protecting us. You were protecting your comfort."

The truth surfaced only when the child, now a teenager, reached out. Olivia felt she had been living in a marriage with missing chapters.

The turning point came when Jack finally said:

"You're right. I robbed you of the truth. And I can't undo that."

It was not a moment of repair, but of clarity—the first step toward honesty, whatever path came next.

Lessons for Couples

- Withholding major truths destroys the foundation of trust.
- Secrets eventually surface, often with far greater damage.
- Repair requires complete transparency and accountability.
- Both partners must decide whether the relationship can withstand the truth.

Lessons for Therapists

- Explore the emotional drivers behind long-term secrecy.
- Support the betrayed partner in processing shock and grief.
- Help couples rebuild communication from a place of truth, not fear.
- Avoid rushing reconciliation; clarity must come first.

Falling in Love Again After Forty Years

Margaret and Henry entered the room slowly, not with conflict but with a quiet sort of sadness—the grief of two people who had shared a life, raised children, survived losses, and somehow lost them along the way. They sat close, but their hands remained in their laps, as though unsure whether they still had permission to reach for each other.

Margaret sighed.

"We talk about bills, grandkids, routines. But when did we stop talking about us?"

Henry nodded, his voice gentle but resigned.

"I thought routine meant stability. I didn't realise it meant we were drifting."

Therapy became an exploration of the small rituals they had abandoned—morning tea in bed, slow dances in the kitchen, Sunday walks holding hands. Their turning point came when Henry said:

"I don't want to just be your husband. I want to be your companion again."

It was the beginning of a rediscovery.

Lessons for Couples

- Long relationships need regular renewal.
- Stability without emotional connection becomes loneliness.
- Small rituals of closeness matter.
- Rediscovering each other requires curiosity, not blame.

Lessons for Therapists

- Honour the length and history of the relationship.
- Explore what the connection looked like before the drift.
- Encourage rebuilding through tiny, consistent rituals.
- Normalise the need to re-learn each other after decades together.

Starting Honest in Later Life

David and Simon, both in their sixties, walked in with quiet confidence, sitting close, knees touching—two men determined not to repeat the mistakes of their past relationships. They were not in therapy because something was broken. They were here to ensure it stayed unbroken.

Simon smiled.

"I don't want to waste time. Let's put everything on the table now—health, finances, intimacy, expectations."

David chuckled.

"Most people wait until they're on the verge of splitting up. We're here on date seven."

Their work became about clarity: what commitment meant now, how to blend families who might not approve, how to maintain autonomy while building closeness. The turning point came when Simon said:

"For the first time in my life, I want to love someone with my eyes wide open."

Lessons for Couples

- Early transparency builds long-term trust.

- Later-life relationships carry complex histories.
- Open conversations prevent avoidable conflict.
- Mature love thrives on honesty, not fantasy.

Lessons for Therapists

- Celebrate proactive therapy.
- Explore expectations shaped by past relationships.
- Encourage full disclosure around health and finances.
- Support couples navigating family dynamics in later life.

The Care Burden

Michael arrived looking worn, his shoulders slumped, keys still in hand as though he had rushed from yet another obligation. Helen followed, equally exhausted, but carrying a different weight—the weight of watching her husband give everything to everyone but her.

Michael sighed.

"I'm the only one who takes care of Mum. My siblings disappear when it's inconvenient."

Helen added quietly:

"And you disappear too. Not physically, emotionally. I miss you."

Michael's loyalty came from love and guilt; Helen's resentment came from love and loneliness. The turning point happened when Helen said:

"I don't want less of your mother. I want more of you."

For the first time, Michael saw that caregiving did not have to mean choosing one family over another—only choosing balance.

Lessons for Couples

- Care responsibilities must be shared or negotiated.

- Resentment grows when one partner carries all the emotional labour.
- Boundaries protect relationships.
- Couples must face caregiving as a team, not as individuals.

Lessons for Therapists

- Map the family's caregiving roles.
- Support guilt without letting it dictate behaviour.
- Help couples set realistic expectations.
- Encourage collaborative caregiving plans.

When Desire Ages at Different Speeds

Evan entered first, his posture confident but eyes shadowed—a man trying hard not to show how deeply rejection had begun to sting. Julia, twenty years younger, followed behind him, moving carefully as though each step carried the weight of unspoken guilt. They sat close, but their bodies faced different directions—a quiet symbol of the mismatch they had come to address.

Julia's voice trembled.

"I love him. But I don't want sex like I used to. I don't even understand why. It's not him… I just feel overwhelmed."

Evan swallowed hard.

"I'm fifty-eight. She's thirty-eight. Everyone assumes I'm the one who'll lose libido first. But it's her. And I don't know how to handle that without sounding needy or pathetic."

Julia wiped her eyes.

"When he reaches for me, I freeze. Not because I don't want him, but because I feel pressure. Like every no is hurting him."

Evan sighed.

"It is hurting me. I feel rejected. And I'm terrified you'll realise I'm too old for you."

Therapy explored the hidden fears beneath the surface. Evan feared being left behind as Julia outgrew him. Julia feared being perceived as failing him sexually. Both were silently suffering—one from longing, one from pressure.

The turning point came when Julia whispered:

"I'm scared you'll think you chose the wrong woman… but I'm still choosing you."

Evan exhaled, his shoulders softening for the first time in months.

And when Evan finally admitted, "I want you—but more than that, I want you comfortable," the pressure that had suffocated Julia began to lift.

Together, they rebuilt intimacy gently—touch without expectation, conversations without defensiveness, connection without demand. They learned that desire does not disappear; it simply needs space, patience, and emotional safety to return.

Lessons for Couples

- Age gaps do not doom relationships—unspoken fears do.
- Libido is not a measure of love; pressure kills desire faster than distance.
- Emotional safety must be rebuilt before sexual intimacy can grow again.
- Connection thrives when partners replace assumptions with honest dialogue.

Lessons for Therapists

- Explore age-gap insecurities from both sides—fear of ageing and fear of inadequacy.
- Normalise fluctuating libido without pathologising either partner.
- Support couples in creating non-sexual closeness as a foundation for desire.
- Address shame, performance pressure, and cultural expectations around sex and age.

The Shouty Fan

Joanne sat stiffly on the sofa, hands clasped so tightly her knuckles whitened. Colin slumped beside her, his face flushed, eyes darting anywhere except towards her. The air carried the residue of last night's match—not the score but the shouting that followed it.

Colin muttered:

"It's just football. I get worked up, that's all. Everyone does."

Joanne shook her head.

"When you scream at the TV, it doesn't feel like just football. I'm right there. I feel like a child again—scared and small."

Colin frowned, suddenly unsure of himself.

"I didn't think it affected you… I thought it stayed in the living room."

Therapy revealed that Colin wasn't truly angry at the team—he was venting at life, at pressure, at what he couldn't control. But Joanne's past trauma meant raised voices pierced straight through her nervous system.

The turning point came when Colin finally whispered:

"I never wanted to be the reason you felt unsafe."

Lessons for Couples

- Old triggers can be reignited in harmless settings.
- Raised voices affect the atmosphere long after the moment passes.
- Naming fear is the first step to reducing it.
- Emotional safety must be prioritised over habits or hobbies.

Lessons for Therapists

- Explore clients' histories with anger and raised voices.
- Help partners understand the nervous system's role in fear responses.
- Highlight the difference between passion and intimidation.
- Support the couple in building agreed-upon de-escalation strategies.

The Friendship Circle

Emma and Laura entered quietly, their bodies angled slightly away from each other despite walking hand in hand. On the sofa, Emma sat forward; Laura slouched back, arms crossed. The tension wasn't explosive—it was confused, tangled in friendships and blurred lines.

Emma spoke first.

"You laugh more with her than you do with me. And you hide things. That hurts."

Laura rolled her eyes, though her voice betrayed guilt.

"She's just a friend. You're reading too much into it."

But Laura had been withholding small things—inside jokes, long voice notes, an intimacy she did not intend to escalate but also did not want to let go of.

The turning point came when Laura finally admitted:

"I liked the attention. I didn't realise how much it was pushing you out."

The issue wasn't infidelity—it was emotional displacement and a lack of boundaries.

Lessons for Couples

- Emotional closeness with friends needs boundaries.
- Jealousy often signals a lack of transparency, not insecurity.
- Partners must discuss what too close means for them.
- Repair requires acknowledging the emotional ripple effect.

Lessons for Therapists

- Help couples define relationship boundaries explicitly.
- Explore attachment styles influencing jealousy.
- Validate fears without reinforcing possessiveness.
- Assist clients in strengthening communication about outside friendships.

When She Hits Him (Version 2)

Megan laughed as she sat down, a strange lightness in her tone. John followed, shoulders hunched, jaw tight. His eyes darted nervously between Megan and the floor.

Megan waved a hand dismissively.

"I only slap him. He's huge! It doesn't hurt him."

John's voice cracked.

"It doesn't hurt my body. It hurts everything else. I feel humiliated."

Megan's upbringing had normalised lashing out; John's upbringing had normalised silence. Together, their patterns collided into a quiet, devastating form of abuse.

The turning point came when Megan finally saw John's face crumble and whispered:

"I didn't realise it was abuse. I thought it was… nothing."

Lessons for Couples

- Abuse isn't cancelled out by size or gender.
- Normalising violence prevents accountability.
- Emotional impact matters as much as physical harm.

- Genuine change begins with recognition and responsibility.

Lessons for Therapists

- Challenge cultural scripts that excuse female violence.
- Explore childhood modelling of conflict behaviours.
- Promote emotional literacy for both partners.
- Ensure safety planning regardless of gender dynamics.

The Ledger of Wrongs

Naomi sat with perfect posture, her jaw tight, her hands clasped in a rigid knot. Adam sat beside her, shoulders sagging, looking like a man who had apologised a thousand times but never escaped the shadow of his mistakes.

Naomi sighed.

"I can't let things go. I don't know how. Every argument brings up everything he's ever done."

Adam exhaled, defeated.

"It feels like living in a courtroom. I can't move forward when everything I say is used as evidence."

Through therapy, Naomi traced her patterns back to childhood, where her parents recorded every wrongdoing in notebooks meant to teach lessons. She had inherited not just a coping strategy, but a weapon.

The turning point came when Naomi finally whispered:

"I don't want to keep collecting evidence. I want peace."

Lessons for Couples

- Keeping score destroys intimacy over time.

- Letting go requires new habits, not just good intentions.
- Forgiveness frees both partners from emotional debt.
- Repair grows where blame is replaced by curiosity.

Lessons for Therapists

- Explore family-of-origin frameworks around punishment and mistakes.
- Teach conflict resolution that centres on repair, not retribution.
- Encourage emotional regulation before difficult discussions.
- Help clients replace old narratives with healthier relational scripts.

The In-Law Triangle

Laura sat forward, frustration radiating from every gesture. Ben leaned back, arms crossed, torn between the woman he loved and the mother who raised him. The tension in the room was thick—the familiar weight of loyalties stretched too thin.

Laura exhaled sharply.

"Your mum calls every day. She undermines my cooking, my parenting… everything. And you never defend me."

Ben looked down.

"She's just trying to help…"

Laura shook her head.

"No. She's trying to control. And you let her."

Therapy peeled back history: Ben was raised to keep the peace, Laura was raised to speak up.

Their conflict wasn't about his mother—it was about boundaries.

The turning point came when Ben finally admitted:

"I've been so scared of upsetting her… that I've been losing you."

Lessons for Couples

- Boundaries with extended family protect the marriage.
- Silence in the face of disrespect equals complicity.
- Couples must present a united front.
- Peacekeeping should not come at the cost of your partner's well-being.

Lessons for Therapists

- Explore childhood loyalty patterns.
- Help partners set boundaries without guilt.
- Teach assertive communication with extended family.
- Reinforce that protecting the marriage is not betrayal.

Old Trauma, New Love

Samantha sat curled in on herself, shoulders tight, breath shallow. James sat beside her, hands clasped, wanting to help but terrified he would do it wrong. The space between them held the shadow of her past—a childhood marked by abuse that still lived inside her skin.

Samantha whispered:

"When he touches me… sometimes my whole body panics. I hate that it happens. I hate that he thinks it's about him."

James swallowed hard.

"I just want to hold you, but I feel like the enemy."

Therapy helped James see that Samantha didn't need rescuing or fury on her behalf; she needed safety, patience, and presence.

The turning point came when James said softly:

"I can't erase what happened. But I can walk beside you while you heal."

Lessons for Couples

- Trauma affects intimacy long after the event.
- Patience builds bridges that force never can.
- Healing happens in safety, not pressure.

- Partners must learn to comfort without rescuing.

Lessons for Therapists

- Prioritise grounding before intimacy work.
- Validate partner anger while redirecting it.
- Teach trauma-informed touch and pacing.
- Support couples through shame, fear, and miscommunication.

When Grief Returns

Mark's grief arrived years after everyone thought he was "fine." Rachel felt shut out, competing with memories she could never soothe. They sat quietly, both exhausted—him from feeling, her from guessing.

Rachel looked at him, voice trembling.

"It feels like she's still here. I can't fight a ghost."

Mark rubbed his forehead.

"I thought I was over it… but lately, she's everywhere in my head. I'm sorry. I don't want this."

Therapy revealed that old grief does not vanish—it waits for triggers, anniversaries, and life changes.

The turning point came when Mark finally said:

"I don't want to go backwards. I just don't know how to move forward."

Rachel took his hand.

"Then let's move forward together."

Lessons for Couples

- Old grief can resurface unexpectedly.
- Partners need clarity, not silence.
- Grief shared is grief softened.
- You can love someone and still mourn someone else.

Lessons for Therapists

- Normalise delayed grief reactions.
- Explore triggers without judgement.
- Teach couples to talk about grief without comparison.
- Support joint rituals for healing and remembrance.

When Violence Is Denied

Jack walked in, insisting he was not "violent," only "loud." Emma's eyes told a different story—wide, alert, trained to anticipate his moods. They sat far apart, the distance a silent consequence of raised voices and hidden fear.

Emma whispered:

"When you shout, I flinch. You say it's not violence… but my body thinks it is."

Jack shook his head.

"I'm not dangerous. I just get angry. People shout. That's normal."

Therapy unpacked denial, fear, and the blurred lines between emotional safety and emotional aggression.

The turning point came when Jack finally saw Emma crying silently beside him.

"I didn't know my voice could do that to you. I thought as long as I didn't hit… I wasn't hurting you."

Lessons for Couples

- Emotional intimidation is real harm.
- Denial delays growth.

- Safety matters more than intention.
- Change begins with acknowledging impact.

Lessons for Therapists

- Clarify distinctions between anger, intimidation, and abuse.
- Help clients recognise nervous-system responses in their partners.
- Challenge minimisation with compassion.
- Prioritise safety planning and self-regulation skills.

The Silent Punishment

Mia walked in first, eyes tired, shoulders tight, her whole body carrying the weight of conversations that never happened. Tom followed slowly, hands in his pockets, avoiding eye contact—the posture of a man who would rather disappear into quiet than face conflict head-on. They sat together, but the space between them pulsed with unspoken resentment.

Mia's voice wavered.

"He doesn't shout. He doesn't argue. He just… shuts down. For days. He walks past me like I'm invisible."

Tom stared at the floor.

"I'm not trying to hurt her. I just don't know what to say. I go quiet so we don't fight."

Mia shook her head, tears gathering.

"It is a fight. Only I'm the only one in it. Your silence feels like punishment."

Tom had grown up in a home where conflict meant retreat, where silence was safety. Mia came from a family where problems were dealt with immediately—voices raised, then hugs followed. Their two worlds collided whenever tension surfaced.

Therapy helped Tom see that withdrawal wasn't neutral—it created anxiety, self-doubt, and loneliness.

The turning point came when Tom finally said:

"I thought staying quiet was protecting us. I didn't realise you heard it as rejection."

Mia exhaled, her shoulders softening for the first time.

"I don't need big speeches. I just need you present."

Together, they began building new habits—timed check-ins, "pause not punish" breaks, and small sentences to replace disappearing: "I need space, but I'm not leaving you."

Lessons for Couples

- Silence can wound as deeply as anger.
- Withdrawal is often a learned behaviour, not malice, but still painful.
- Repair requires presence, even in small amounts.
- Clear communication prevents the space for abandonment.

Lessons for Therapists

- Explore family-of-origin conflict styles.
- Teach structured time-outs that soothe rather than punish.
- Help partners create language for emotional shutdowns.

- Reframe withdrawal as a skill deficit, not a character flaw.

"Money reveals what words often conceal: fear, insecurity, and longing."

Money as Control

Carla perched on the edge of the chair, her hands twisting the sleeve of her jumper. Paul sat back, defeated, exhaustion etched across his face. The silence between them was thick with unpaid bills and unspoken fears.

Carla trembled.

"I spent the money. All of it. I kept thinking I'd fix it before you found out."

Paul stared at her.

"You gambled our future on shopping. Trinkets. Things that meant nothing."

Therapy uncovered painful truths—Carla used spending to soothe anxiety, to fill loneliness, to feel momentarily alive. But secrecy had turned it into control.

The turning point came when Carla said:

"I wasn't trying to control us. I was trying to escape myself."

Lessons for Couples

- Financial secrecy is emotional betrayal.

- Spending often masks deeper distress.
- Transparency rebuilds trust slowly.
- Shared plans create safety.

Lessons for Therapists

- Explore emotional triggers behind spending patterns.
- Address power imbalances around money.
- Teach practical tools for financial honesty.
- Support couples through consequences and repair.

"Sometimes the battlefield isn't home—it's childhood."

Parenting Styles Clash

Olivia sat upright, arms folded, her frustration bubbling close to the surface. Dan leaned back, tense, jaw clenched—the picture of discipline waiting to happen. Their battle wasn't with each other but with the ghosts of their upbringing.

Dan growled:

"They'll never learn discipline if you give in to every whim."

Olivia snapped back:

"And they'll never feel safe if you terrify them!"

Therapy revealed the truth: Olivia grew up under harsh rules; Dan with none. Their extremes met in the middle—in their children.

The turning point came when Dan said:

"We're not our parents. We get to choose differently."

Lessons for Couples

- Parenting differences come from childhood experiences.
- Children need both safety and boundaries.
- Unity requires compromise, not competition.
- Change begins with self-awareness.

Lessons for Therapists

- Map each partner's family history.
- Highlight how extremes clash.
- Support the development of shared parenting values.
- Reinforce positive co-parenting communication.

The Gambling Secret

Anthony sat slumped, eyes hollow, hands trembling. Maria sat rigid beside him, her face pale with shock and betrayal. Between them lay a truth that had shattered everything: their home wasn't theirs. It had not been for years.

Maria whispered:

"You let me dream of Portugal. Of retirement. Of a future. And it was all a lie?"

Anthony's voice cracked.

"I couldn't stop. And every time I tried to tell you, I froze. I was ashamed."

The turning point came when Anthony finally admitted:

"I wasn't protecting you. I was hiding from myself."

Their future was uncertain. Therapy focused on harm reduction, accountability, and whether trust could ever be rebuilt.

Lessons for Couples

- Gambling secrets destroy financial and emotional security.

- Shame fuels secrecy and denial.
- Recovery requires honesty, structure, and support.
- Trust rebuilds slowly—if at all.

Lessons for Therapists

- Assess financial safety and risk immediately.
- Explore the emotional drivers of addictive behaviour.
- Support realistic decision-making around repair.
- Provide resources for gambling recovery pathways.

Battling the In-Laws

Rachel walked in with her shoulders tight, frustration radiating beneath her calm exterior. Luke followed behind, eyes weary, the look of a man stretched thin between two women he loved. They sat close, but the tension between them was unmistakable—shaped by years of interference from Luke's mother and Rachel's exhaustion from feeling unwelcome in her own family.

Rachel's voice broke.

"She treats me like I'm an outsider. She criticises everything I do. I dread family dinners."

Luke rubbed his hands together.

"She just wants to help… she doesn't mean it badly."

Rachel shook her head.

"I'm not asking you to choose her or me. I'm asking you to stop letting her tear us apart."

The pattern was old: Luke avoided conflict, hoping peace would magically return. Rachel felt abandoned every time he stayed silent.

The turning point came when Luke finally said:

"I can't keep pretending nothing's wrong. I need to protect our marriage—not everyone's feelings."

For the first time, Rachel felt chosen.

Lessons for Couples

- Avoiding conflict with in-laws creates deeper conflict at home.
- Partners must stand together as a unified team.
- Boundaries preserve relationships; silence erodes them.
- Loyalty to parents must not overwrite loyalty to the marriage.

Lessons for Therapists

- Explore the family-of-origin dynamics fuelling avoidance.
- Help partners create actionable, respectful boundaries.
- Validate the emotional injury caused by triangulation.
- Role-play difficult conversations when one partner fears confrontation.

The Ex Idealised

Charlotte entered the room with a sadness that clung to her like a shadow. Daniel followed, jaw tight, carrying the unspoken fear that he would never be enough. They sat together, but the emotional distance stretched wide—filled with memories of her late partner, a man she once planned to leave but later romanticised after his death.

Charlotte stared at her hands.

"Since he died… I only remember the good bits. I know we had problems, but grief makes everything blurry."

Daniel swallowed hard.

"I can't compete with a dead man who's been rewritten as perfect."

Therapy helped Charlotte explore the guilt she carried—guilt that made her silence the truth of her past relationship and project idealised memories into her present.

The turning point came when Charlotte whispered:

"I've been grieving the man I wish he were… not the man he actually was. And that's not fair to you."

Daniel finally exhaled. For the first time, he wasn't fighting a ghost—he was being seen by the woman sitting in front of him.

Lessons for Couples

- Grief can distort memory and idealise past relationships.
- Present partners need honesty, not romanticised comparisons.
- Healing requires balancing remembrance with reality.
- New love cannot grow in the shadow of unresolved grief.

Lessons for Therapists

- Normalise idealisation after loss without endorsing it.
- Encourage clients to remember full, balanced narratives.
- Support partners in expressing insecurity without shame.
- Help couples separate grief work from relationship work.

A Hidden Truth

Samantha sat stiffly, eyes rimmed red, hands twisting a tissue as though trying to wring the truth out of it. Paul sat beside her, shoulders hunched, the weight of years of secrecy pressing down on him. The space between them pulsed with shock and betrayal—the kind that changes the shape of a marriage overnight.

Samantha's voice cracked:

"You had encounters with men… and you hid it from me. For years."

Paul stared at the floor.

"I didn't know how to tell you. It didn't change how I felt about you. I was confused… ashamed."

To Samantha, the betrayal wasn't about sexuality—it was the deception.

For Paul, the secrecy had been a cage he didn't know how to open.

The turning point came when Samantha said softly:

"I can handle the truth. I just needed you to trust me with it."

For Paul, it was the doorway out of shame.

For Samantha, it was the beginning of rebuilding honesty on new terms.

Lessons for Couples

- Sexual confusion is not betrayal—secrecy is.
- Trust requires truth, even when it's uncomfortable.
- Identity shifts must be faced together, not hidden.
- Openness allows couples to renegotiate closeness on honest ground.

Lessons for Therapists

- Create space for sexuality discussions without judgement.
- Help partners separate identity from deceit.
- Support the betrayed partner in processing shock safely.
- Facilitate slow, transparent rebuilding of trust.

Love Across Colour Lines

Ella and Marcus entered holding hands, yet the strain showed in their eyes. Their love was strong, but the pressure from both families was wearing them thin. Ella's parents pretended Marcus didn't exist. Marcus's family dismissed Ella as someone who would never understand their struggles. Their relationship wasn't failing—the world around them was.

Ella spoke first, her voice trembling.

"My family act like you're invisible. It's humiliating."

Marcus nodded slowly.

"And mine smile at you while whispering behind your back. You don't deserve that."

Therapy uncovered the exhaustion of constantly defending their love—not from each other, but from people who should have supported them.

The turning point came when Marcus said:

"We can't change our families. But we can stop letting them decide how we feel about each other."

Ella squeezed his hand—a quiet promise that they would face the world together, not separately.

Lessons for Couples

- External prejudice puts enormous strain on interracial relationships.
- Unity and communication protect the couple from outside judgement.
- Families may never change—but boundaries can.
- Love grows strongest when partners choose each other daily.

Lessons for Therapists

- Validate the emotional burden of societal and familial prejudice.
- Explore cultural identity, pride, and misunderstanding with care.
- Help couples build protective boundaries around their relationship.

- Encourage shared rituals that strengthen connection against external pressure.

When Jealousy Consumes

Chloe arrived tense, shoulders raised, eyes sharp with suspicion. Liam followed, exhausted, his movements slow, as though dragged down by months of defending himself against things he had never done. They sat at opposite ends of the sofa, their bodies mirroring the distance between truth and fear.

Chloe said quietly:

"I check his phone, his mileage, his social media. I can't help it. I keep waiting for him to do what my dad did to my mum."

Liam rubbed his temples.

"I've never given her a reason. Not once. But she treats me like a criminal. She even accused me of flirting with my cousin."

Chloe swallowed hard.

"I don't want to be this person. But if I stop checking… I panic."

Therapy explored inherited beliefs—Chloe's mother had warned her that all men cheat eventually. Her fear wasn't about Liam; it was about childhood wounds still echoing loudly.

The turning point came when Chloe whispered:

"I'm punishing you for someone else's sins."

Lessons for Couples

- Jealousy often arises from past wounds, not present behaviour.
- Constant suspicion erodes trust on both sides.
- Transparency helps, but reassurance alone cannot heal childhood fears.
- Healing requires challenging the stories we inherited about relationships.

Lessons for Therapists

- Explore family-of-origin narratives about betrayal and loyalty.
- Support the anxious partner in developing internal safety.
- Help the other partner set compassionate boundaries around privacy.

- Teach couples how to separate memory from current reality.

The Emotional Affair

Emma entered with a heaviness that clung to her shoulders. Daniel followed, eyes wounded but angry, his jaw tight. They sat close but angled away, the tension saturated with hurt, longing, and confusion.

Emma said softly:

"I didn't sleep with him. But I told him things I stopped telling you."

Daniel replied:

"That's intimacy. You shared your hopes and fears with him. Those belonged to us."

Emma's "friendship" with a colleague had slowly shifted into emotional dependency. There were no stolen kisses—just stolen closeness. She loved the attention, the listening ear, the ease.

But Daniel felt displaced.

"I felt like a placeholder," he said. "Like you saved your best self for him."

The turning point came when Emma admitted:

"He listened because he wasn't living the messy parts of life with me. You were. I forgot that mattered."

Lessons for Couples

- Emotional infidelity often hurts more deeply than physical affairs.
- Vulnerability shared outside the relationship erodes trust.
- Repair requires transparency and boundaries around friendships.
- Rebuilding connection means choosing each other intentionally every day.

Lessons for Therapists

- Clarify the definition of emotional versus physical infidelity.
- Explore unmet needs without framing them as excuses.
- Support couples in renegotiating boundaries.
- Guide clients to rebuild emotional intimacy within the relationship.

Pornography's Grip

Hannah sat stiffly, hands clenched. David stared at the floor, shame radiating from him like heat. They had not touched in months—silence had built a wall neither knew how to climb.

Hannah said:

"You'd rather have a screen than me. Do you know how small that makes me feel?"

David swallowed.

"It's not about you. It's just… easier. There's no pressure."

What began as stress relief had become replacement—hours lost, intimacy avoided, self-esteem shattered.

The turning point came when David said:

"I didn't realise how much I'd disappeared from us."

Lessons for Couples

- Excessive porn use can replace connection instead of enhancing it.
- Avoidance deepens insecurity and distance.
- Healing requires honest conversations about needs and pressure.

- Reconnection flourishes with gentleness and patience.

Lessons for Therapists

- Avoid moralising—focus on impact, not judgement.
- Explore whether porn is stress relief, dissociation, or avoidance.
- Support rebuilding trust and sexual confidence.
- Encourage gradual reconnection rather than forced intimacy.

Work as Escape

Sarah walked in looking exhausted, as though she had been raising the world alone. Luke followed, defensive, laptop bag still slung over his shoulder, the smell of stale office air clinging to him.

Sarah said:

"You give the best of yourself to work. We get the leftovers."

Luke sighed.

"I'm providing for us. Isn't that enough?"

But it wasn't about money—it was about presence. Luke stayed late to avoid the stress at home, telling himself he was doing it for his family while quietly avoiding them.

The turning point came when Sarah whispered:

"They don't want your money. They want their dad."

Luke finally heard what she had been saying for years.

Lessons for Couples

- Overworking can hide deeper avoidance or overwhelm.
- Families need presence more than financial provision.

- Resentment builds when one partner carries the emotional load alone.
- Connection grows when partners share responsibilities and emotional labour.

Lessons for Therapists

- Explore what work represents—identity, escape, safety, or avoidance.
- Validate the working partner's stress while addressing the impact.
- Encourage dialogue around shared expectations.
- Support plans for rebalancing time, presence, and emotional attention.

The Unspoken Expectations

Leah walked in first, her shoulders tight, the kind of stiff posture that comes from years of carrying invisible loads. Mark followed, his neck craning forward, his expression confused rather than defensive. They sat close, yet the distance between them was built from unspoken expectations neither had ever dared to express.

Leah spoke quietly.

"I do everything. The house, the kids, the schedules. He helps... but only if I ask. Why do I have to ask?"

Mark frowned.

"I'm not a mind reader. I don't want to get it wrong, so I wait for instructions. That's not me being lazy. That's me trying to keep the peace."

Leah looked down.

"It feels like I'm his mother, not his wife."

Therapy revealed a familiar cycle. Leah expected Mark to "just know," while Mark waited for clarity. Both felt unappreciated.

The turning point came when Mark said:

"I wasn't raised to see what needs doing. But I'm willing to learn, if you can teach me without hating me for not already knowing."

Leah's shoulders finally softened.

It was the first moment she saw willingness instead of resistance.

Lessons for Couples

- Unspoken expectations breed resentment.
- Clarity is not control; it is collaboration.
- Change requires willingness, not perfection.
- Appreciation keeps effort alive.

Lessons for Therapists

- Explore each partner's family-of-origin roles around chores and mental load.
- Normalise differences between noticing tasks and awaiting direction.
- Teach couples practical communication scripts.
- Reinforce that resentment is a signal, not a solution.

When Touch Disappears

Michelle sat rigid on the sofa, arms wrapped around her middle as if holding herself together. Tom sat with his legs apart, hands clasped, staring at the floor, shame clinging to him like a shadow. They looked like two people who belonged together, yet had not touched in months.

Michelle whispered:

"He doesn't hold my hand anymore. Doesn't kiss me. Doesn't even brush past me in the kitchen. I feel invisible."

Tom swallowed hard.

"I don't know how to start again. I stopped touching her because I felt rejected. Then she felt rejected. Now... I'm scared to try."

Their home had become silent, not just in sound, but in touch. Therapy helped them explore the deeper truth. Emotional hurts from old arguments had slowly calcified into physical distance.

The turning point came when Tom said:

"I didn't stop touching you because I stopped loving you. I stopped because I didn't know if I was still wanted."

Michelle reached across the space between them, the first touch they had shared in sessions, and whispered:

"I've been waiting for you to try."

Lessons for Couples

- Physical affection is connection, not merely intimacy.
- Touch withers when emotional safety is lost.
- Rebuilding closeness starts with small, consistent gestures.
- Avoidance grows when partners fear rejection.

Lessons for Therapists

- Explore the emotional injuries behind the loss of touch.
- Use gradual exposure to rebuild physical connection.
- Normalise anxiety around initiating affection.
- Support couples in co-creating safe routines of closeness.

"Love bends, but it breaks when one partner carries all the strain."

When One Partner Becomes the Parent

Jo arrived exhausted, dark crescents beneath her eyes, her movements slow and heavy. Ben followed with a bounce in his step, chatting about trivial things, masking the deeper issues he did not want to face. They sat side by side, but their roles were painfully clear. She was the adult. He was the child.

Jo sighed.

"I feel like his mother. I manage the bills, the appointments, the house… everything. He's 38. I shouldn't have to do this."

Ben shrugged.

"I'm just easy-going. She's the organised one. It works."

Jo's jaw tightened.

"It doesn't work. I'm drowning."

Therapy revealed Ben's lifelong pattern of avoidance. His mother had done everything for him. Jo had stepped into the same role without realising it, until resentment took root.

The turning point came when Jo burst into tears and said:

"I want a partner. Not another person to look after."

For the first time, Ben's expression shifted. He saw not nagging, but pain.

He admitted quietly:

"I thought you wanted to lead. I didn't realise you felt alone."

It was the moment adulthood stopped being optional.

Lessons for Couples

- Parent–child dynamics erode intimacy.
- Responsibility must be shared, not assigned.
- Resentment signals emotional overload.
- Equality requires both partners to step up, not one to step back.

Lessons for Therapists

- Identify parent–child dynamics early.
- Support the avoidant partner in developing adult competencies.
- Encourage the over-functioning partner to relinquish unhealthy control.
- Reinforce boundaries that create partnership, not caretaking.

"A relationship can survive many storms, but not constant interference."

When the In-Laws Become a Third Partner

Emily entered first, shoulders tense, her eyes fixed on the floor as though preparing herself for another battle she had not chosen. Alex walked in behind her, jaw tight, frustration radiating from him like heat. They sat close, yet the distance between them was unmistakable. A tension built not from each other, but from everyone else in their lives.

Emily sighed.

"I can't cope with your mother texting you ten times a day about our decisions. It feels like we're never alone."

Alex rubbed the bridge of his nose.

"She just wants to help. She worries. She's always been involved."

Emily's voice cracked.

"Involved? She vetoed our wedding venue. She has a key to our house. She tells me how to run our home. I feel like the other woman in my own marriage."

Therapy revealed Alex's lifelong role as the compliant son, trained to keep the peace by giving in. Emily was not fighting his mother. She was fighting for her place.

The turning point came when Alex said quietly:

"I've been scared to upset her... but I can't keep losing you in the process."

For the first time, Emily's shoulders loosened. Alex was not choosing sides. He was choosing boundaries.

Lessons for Couples

- Extended family should support the relationship, not sit inside it.
- Boundaries protect love; silence erodes it.
- Loyalty to a partner and respect for parents can coexist.
- Couples must present a united front to reduce interference.

Lessons for Therapists

- Explore family roles and generational expectations.
- Help clients differentiate guilt from responsibility.
- Teach boundary-setting as a relational skill, not a rejection.
- Mediate conversations that reduce triangulation.

When One Retires and the Other Doesn't

Helen walked in briskly, still in her work clothes, the smell of outside air and busyness clinging to her. Peter followed slowly, wearing soft leisurewear, moving with the relaxed rhythm of someone who finally had time. They sat together, but their lives were running at two different speeds. One sprinting, the other strolling.

Peter spoke first.

"I thought retirement would be good for us. But she's never home. I'm lonely."

Helen sighed.

"I'm exhausted. I go to work all day, and when I get home he's waiting for me like I'm his whole social life."

Peter shook his head.

"I just want time with her. Time I never had before."

Therapy explored the shift in identity. Peter was grieving the loss of purpose. Helen was overwhelmed by new pressure. They were not falling out of love. They were adjusting to a new season.

The turning point came when Helen said gently:

"I'm not avoiding you. I'm just tired. If we plan time together, I can give you the best of me, not what's left of me."

Peter nodded, the tension easing.

They began structuring their days instead of colliding through them.

Lessons for Couples

- Retirement affects both partners, even if only one stops working.
- Structured connection protects against resentment.
- Identity shifts require patience and renegotiation.
- Balance grows when both partners have purpose.

Lessons for Therapists

- Explore identity loss, not just relationship conflict.
- Encourage independent routines for the retired partner.
- Help the working partner set boundaries without guilt.
- Support couples in designing a shared vision of this new chapter.

The Hidden Addiction

Maya entered slowly, her shoulders drawn inwards, the look of a woman carrying a truth too heavy for one person. Ethan followed, restless and agitated, fingers tapping his knee in sharp bursts. They sat together, both trying to hold the pieces of a life shaken by revelations neither wanted to face.

Maya spoke in a trembling voice.

"I didn't know he'd started gambling again. The savings... the lies... I feel like I don't know who I'm married to."

Ethan stared at the floor.

"I didn't mean to hide it. I just... couldn't stop. And I didn't want to disappoint her."

Maya whispered:

"You didn't disappoint me. You scared me."

Therapy peeled back layers of shame, secrecy, and cravings. Ethan was not dishonest by nature. He was drowning and terrified of being seen struggling.

The turning point came when Ethan said quietly:

"I don't need forgiveness first. I need help."

For Maya, it was the first time she heard accountability instead of excuses. For Ethan, it was the first time he stopped running.

Lessons for Couples

- Addiction thrives in secrecy and shame.
- Recovery starts with honesty, not promises.
- Partners need boundaries, not blame.
- Trust rebuilds through consistent action, not grand gestures.

Lessons for Therapists

- Address the addiction and the relationship patterns around it.
- Normalise relapse without minimising harm.
- Guide partners in creating safety plans and financial boundaries.
- Encourage external support through groups, treatment, and accountability structures.

"When one person carries all the guilt, the relationship buckles under the weight."

The Weight of Blame

Evelyn sat stiffly on the sofa, back straight, eyes fixed on the carpet as if waiting for judgement. Her partner, Russell, hovered at the edge of his seat, shoulders rounded, a man worn down by years of trying to fix what he barely understood. The air between them felt strained, the kind of tension that forms when one partner always apologises and the other never stops bracing for the next mistake.

Evelyn spoke first, her voice barely above a whisper.

"I take the blame for everything. If he's stressed, it's my fault. If the kids argue, it's my fault. If dinner burns, it's my fault."

Russell shook his head.

"I'm not blaming you. I'm just tired. And sometimes you take things too personally."

But therapy revealed the deeper pattern. Evelyn had grown up in a household where keeping the peace meant absorbing all the blame. Russell had grown used to letting her take it.

The turning point came when Evelyn said softly:

"I don't want to be the scapegoat anymore. I want to be your partner."

For the first time, Russell realised the cost of the peace he had unknowingly relied upon.

Lessons for Couples

- Blame imbalance creates emotional exhaustion.
- Peacekeeping should not mean self-sacrifice.
- Real partnership requires shared responsibility.
- Defensiveness blocks connection and repair.

Lessons for Therapists

- Explore childhood patterns around blame and responsibility.
- Help rediscover balanced accountability.
- Challenge automatic blaming behaviours gently but firmly.
- Support the quieter partner in reclaiming emotional space.

*"When parents split loyalty down the middle, children feel
broken on both sides."*

Caught in the Middle

Tom entered with the posture of a man carrying decades of tension in his shoulders. His ex-partner, Lydia, followed with her arms folded tightly, jaw clenched, the familiar armour of someone preparing for battle. Though no longer a couple, they sat far apart, joined only by their ten-year-old daughter, Isla, whose emotional wellbeing sat squarely between them.

Tom spoke first.

"Isla comes back from Lydia's in tears. She says I'm the reason we split. I never said anything like that."

Lydia's eyes flashed.

"I'm trying to protect her. She needs to know the truth."

Therapy revealed that both were projecting their hurt onto their daughter. Tom through over-permissiveness. Lydia through over-sharing. The child was not choosing sides. She was drowning in adult feelings.

The turning point came when Lydia whispered:

"I didn't realise I was making her carry my pain."

Lessons for Couples (and Co-Parents)

- Children should not be messengers or emotional buffers.
- Loyalty conflicts create long-term emotional harm.
- Co-parents must separate their hurt from their parenting.
- Children thrive on neutrality, not pressure.

Lessons for Therapists

- Reinforce child-centred communication.
- Identify indirect emotional burdening.
- Encourage co-parenting boundaries around adult topics.
- Help each parent process grief without involving the child.

Letting the Nest Open

Harriet walked into the room with tear-bright eyes, clutching a diary she had kept since her daughters were toddlers. Her husband, Colin, followed slowly, shoulders slumped, his expression torn between relief and regret. Their youngest had just left for university, leaving a silence at home too loud to ignore.

Harriet spoke first.

"I don't know who I am without the girls. My whole life has been about being their mum."

Colin exhaled heavily.

"I tried to tell you to make time for yourself years ago, but you wouldn't. And now… now you're angry at me."

Harriet bit her lip.

"I'm not angry. I'm lost."

Therapy explored identity foreclosure. Harriet had been so consumed by mothering that she had no sense of self beyond it. Colin, meanwhile, felt punished for something he had no control over.

The turning point came when Harriet admitted:

"I thought being needed made me valuable. But maybe being me is enough."

Lessons for Couples

- Empty-nest transitions can magnify identity loss.
- Couples must renegotiate roles and closeness.
- Personal growth strengthens, not threatens, a relationship.
- Identity shifts require patience and compassion.

Lessons for Therapists

- Explore identity beyond parenting roles.
- Support partners in rediscovering individual passions.
- Normalise grief around changing family dynamics.
- Encourage couples to rebuild connection intentionally.

"Avoidance doesn't protect love; it starves it."

The Fear of Difficult Conversations

Megan sat perched on the edge of the sofa, fingers twisting the zip of her hoodie, eyes fixed on a spot on the floor. Tom sat beside her, arms crossed, his jaw tight in that familiar way that said he had given up trying to be heard. They sat close, but their silence revealed how far apart they felt. Two people who loved each other deeply, yet had become frightened of speaking the truth.

Megan finally muttered:

"I don't bring things up because I don't want to start a row."

Tom sighed.

"But not talking about it starts a row anyway. You shut down, and I feel shut out."

Megan had grown up in a home where conflict meant shouting, slammed doors, and days of cold silence. Avoidance had always felt safer than honesty. But in her marriage, silence became the very thing that eroded connection.

The turning point came when Megan whispered:

"I thought keeping quiet kept the peace… but it's killing us."

Therapy helped her understand that avoiding hard conversations was not protecting the relationship. It was starving it. Slowly, safety grew around small, honest exchanges.

Lessons for Couples

- Avoidance creates distance, even when the intention is peace.
- Conflict handled gently strengthens a relationship.
- Truth told kindly is safer than silence that festers.
- Emotional safety grows through small, consistent honesty.

Lessons for Therapists

- Explore clients' early experiences of conflict.
- Teach structured communication to reduce fear.
- Normalise discomfort in difficult conversations.
- Reinforce that repair becomes possible only after openness.

Constant Criticism, Constant Defence

Priya sat stiffly, her lips pressed together, eyes darting towards her husband as if bracing for the next comment. Daniel sat upright, irritation flickering across his face. Not anger, but exasperation, the kind that builds when someone feels misunderstood. The atmosphere felt brittle, ready to crack under the weight of years of miscommunication.

Priya said quietly:

"He's always correcting me. How I cook, how I drive, even how I breathe sometimes."

Daniel shook his head.

"I'm trying to help. If I don't say anything, things go wrong."

Therapy revealed something deeper. Daniel had grown up in a household where criticism was the only form of guidance. Priya, however, had experienced constant criticism as rejection. Neither was wrong, but neither was being heard.

The turning point came when Daniel admitted:

"I didn't realise my 'helping' was the thing hurting us."

That moment cracked open empathy. Priya softened. Daniel began to listen differently.

Lessons for Couples

- Criticism often masks fear, not superiority.
- Defensiveness blocks connection.
- Replacing criticism with curiosity rebuilds safety.
- Couples must learn each other's emotional history.

Lessons for Therapists

- Translate criticism into underlying needs.
- Help partners hear themes, not just tone.
- Teach softer entry points for feedback.
- Support clients in developing mutual empathy.

Drifting Apart Without Realising

Elise walked in with a soft, tired smile, the kind worn by someone who had kept going out of habit rather than passion. Mark followed slowly, hands deep in his pockets, looking like a man who still cared but had no idea how to fix what he could not name. They sat politely, like colleagues rather than partners. Two lives running parallel, but no longer touching.

Elise explained:

"We stopped talking about anything real. We talk about bills, work, the kids… but not us."

Mark rubbed the back of his neck.

"I didn't realise how far we drifted until she said she felt lonely."

Neither had betrayed the other. Neither had lied. Their relationship had simply softened into something functional. A partnership without connection.

The turning point came when Mark said:

"I don't want to lose you because we forgot to pay attention."

Therapy focused on rebuilding micro-connection. Moments of eye contact, small gestures, intentional time. They did not need fireworks. They needed presence.

Lessons for Couples

- Drifting happens slowly and silently.
- Connection must be intentional.
- Small daily efforts rebuild closeness.
- Loneliness within a relationship is a call for reconnection, not blame.

Lessons for Therapists

- Highlight the slow erosion, not just the crisis.
- Encourage rituals of connection.
- Normalise seasons of disconnection.
- Help couples rebuild curiosity about each other.

"When people stop feeling seen, they start feeling alone."

Lost in the Busy

Emma walked in first, blazer still on, phone still in her hand, as though she had sprinted there straight from a meeting. Her energy buzzed with exhaustion rather than purpose. Tom followed slowly, shoulders heavy, the look of a man who used to be patient but was now frayed around the edges. They sat close, but their bodies leaned in different emotional directions. Together, yet living apart in rhythm.

Emma admitted:

"I don't stop. Work, emails, clients... I barely have time to breathe. I know he feels ignored, but I don't know how to slow down."

Tom sighed.

"I'm proud of her. I really am. But I miss her. I miss us. I feel like I'm bottom of the list."

Emma defended herself reflexively.

"I'm doing it for us. For our future."

Tom shook his head gently.

"But we're losing our present."

Therapy explored Emma's fear of stopping. That stillness might mean failure, or that slowing down would let the pressure catch up with her. Tom was not asking for grand gestures. He wanted presence, not perfection.

The turning point came when Emma whispered:

"I didn't realise being busy made you feel unloved."

Lessons for Couples

- Love needs presence, not productivity.
- Constant busyness erodes connection over time.
- Small, consistent moments of attention build intimacy.
- Shared routines restore closeness more than big gestures.

Lessons for Therapists

- Explore the underlying fear driving overwork.
- Help couples renegotiate time, energy, and priorities.
- Encourage micro-connection rituals such as check-ins and pauses.
- Validate both the strain of pressure and the pain of neglect.

When Loss Turns to Blame

Daniel entered stiffly, his jaw clenched as though holding back words he was not ready to say. His wife, Priya, walked in quietly behind him, her eyes swollen from tears she had cried alone. They sat with a cushion of space between them. Not emotional distance, but fear of causing more harm.

Their infant daughter had died nine months earlier. Since then, every conversation had turned into an argument neither meant to start.

Priya whispered:

"He blames me. He doesn't say it, but I feel it."

Daniel finally spoke, his voice cracking.

"I blame myself. And I don't know where to put it. So it comes out wrong."

Priya sobbed softly.

"We lost the same baby. Why does it feel like we're grieving two different children?"

Therapy helped them name what they were truly fighting. Not each other, but the pain of a future stolen from both of them. Priya grieved quietly, inwardly. Daniel grieved loudly, outwardly. Both felt alone inside the same heartbreak.

The turning point came when Daniel said:

"I'm angry because I don't know how to live without her. Not because of you."

Lessons for Couples

- Grief affects partners differently; neither response is wrong.
- Blame is often misplaced pain seeking direction.
- Joint grief rituals can reconnect grieving partners.
- Vulnerability bridges where anger divides.

Lessons for Therapists

- Normalise divergent grieving styles.
- Teach couples to communicate pain without accusation.
- Support the creation of shared grief practices.
- Help partners rebuild emotional safety after loss.

The Partner Who Keeps Checking

Sarah sat with her coat still on, arms wrapped tightly around herself, as though she needed protection even inside the room. Leo sat beside her, foot tapping rapidly, eyes darting between Sarah and me as if scanning for danger. They looked like a couple who loved each other deeply, but were suffocating under the weight of unspoken fear.

Sarah admitted:

"He checks my phone every night. My messages, my photos… even my bank statement. He says it's because he loves me."

Leo interrupted quickly:

"I've been cheated on before. I just need to know she's not going to leave. I can't go through that again."

Sarah looked down.

"But you're pushing me away by trying to hold on too tightly."

Leo's fear was not anger. It was abandonment. But his behaviours were controlling, slowly eroding the trust he was desperate to protect.

Therapy helped Leo see that reassurance gained through surveillance never lasts. What he needed was healing, not proof. Sarah needed boundaries, not constant suspicion.

The turning point came when Leo whispered:

"I don't want to lose you... but I can't keep you like this."

Lessons for Couples

- Reassurance gained through control is never real reassurance.
- Boundaries protect trust; they do not threaten it.
- Love cannot flourish under surveillance.
- Healing requires the courage to trust again, not proof-checking.

Lessons for Therapists

- Identify fear-based controlling patterns early.
- Work on attachment wounds beneath the behaviours.
- Teach couples balanced transparency, not intrusion.
- Support the controlled partner in reclaiming autonomy safely.

The Battle for the Last Word

Emma sat stiffly, her chin lifted in quiet defiance, as though surrendering even an inch would mean losing something vital. Tom slouched beside her, arms crossed, the posture of a man who had run out of patience long before stepping into the room. The atmosphere buzzed with challenge. Two people who loved each other, yet fought like adversaries in a courtroom.

Emma admitted:

"I can't let things go. I need him to understand every detail of why he's wrong."

Tom shook his head.

"She can argue for hours. And if I don't keep up, she says I'm shutting down."

The pattern was clear. Emma argued for validation. Tom withdrew for peace. Both ended up wounded.

The turning point came when Emma said quietly:

"I think winning has become more important to me than connecting… and I don't like who that makes me."

Lessons for Couples

- Winning an argument often means losing closeness.
- Conflict eases when both partners feel heard, not defeated.
- Stepping back can be healthy; withdrawal is not always avoidance.
- Validation builds bridges where defensiveness builds walls.

Lessons for Therapists

- Identify underlying insecurities disguised as logic.
- Slow down fast thinkers and invite withdrawn partners to re-enter safely.
- Challenge win–lose dynamics gently but firmly.
- Teach communication models that prioritise understanding, not victory.

Married to the Job

Oliver entered wearing his suit jacket like armour, the faint scent of coffee and exhaustion clinging to him. His wife, Jodie, followed, arms folded, her foot tapping lightly. Impatience mixed with heartbreak. They sat close, but the distance between them was filled with missed dinners, unread texts, and one-sided plans.

Oliver rubbed his temples.

"I'm doing this for us. For our future."

Jodie's voice cracked.

"But I'm not in our present."

For years, Oliver had poured everything into climbing the corporate ladder. Jodie had waited, hoping the pace would slow. It never did.

The turning point came when Oliver finally said:

"I thought providing was love. I didn't realise absence felt like abandonment."

Lessons for Couples

- Overworking can become emotional avoidance.

- Providing financially does not replace emotional presence.
- Real connection happens in everyday moments.
- Partners must define success together, not separately.

Lessons for Therapists

- Explore the role of work as coping or distraction.
- Help couples build rituals of connection.
- Normalise conversations about burnout and emotional neglect.
- Support redefining shared priorities beyond productivity.

Affection Withheld

Nina sat perched on the edge of the sofa, hands tucked beneath her legs as if trying to make herself small. Darren sat back, eyes downcast, fingers tapping rhythmically. A man aching for warmth that never seemed to come. The room felt cold, not from temperature, but from months of unspoken loneliness.

Darren sighed.

"She doesn't touch me. Doesn't hug me. I feel invisible."

Nina's eyes watered.

"When I was growing up, touch wasn't safe. It wasn't kind. I shut it off."

Her withdrawal was not rejection. It was protection. Darren's longing was not neediness. It was hunger for connection.

The turning point came when Nina whispered:

"I want to learn how to let you near me… I just don't know how yet."

Lessons for Couples

- Touch histories shape adult intimacy.
- Affection can be relearned with safety and patience.

- Naming needs prevents resentment from building silently.
- Healing requires vulnerability from both partners.

Lessons for Therapists

- Assess trauma or aversion behind withdrawn affection.
- Teach slow, consent-based reconnection exercises.
- Hold space for both partners' fears without judgement.
- Reinforce that progress comes through small, repeated moments of safety.

"When one partner grows, the other must learn how to grow alongside them."

Outgrowing the Old Dynamic

Lydia sat with her hands folded neatly in her lap, posture straight, eyes clear. The quiet confidence of a woman who had finally begun to find herself. Tom slouched beside her, staring at the floor, his leg bouncing with agitation. They looked like two people shifting on different emotional timelines. She expanding, he clinging tightly to the familiar.

Lydia spoke first.

"I'm not the same person I was two years ago. Therapy, work, friendships... I've changed. I've grown. And Tom wants everything to stay exactly the same."

Tom exhaled sharply.

"She's too different now. She doesn't need me like she used to. And I don't know where I fit anymore."

Their story was not one of betrayal or crisis, but of uneven growth. Lydia was flourishing. Tom felt abandoned. Therapy helped them name the imbalance without blame, exploring how to reconnect without forcing Lydia backwards or pushing Tom into panic.

The turning point came when Tom said quietly:

"I'm scared I won't be enough for the version of you that's growing."

Lydia reached for his hand.

"You don't need to be the old version of you. Just be willing to grow with me."

Lessons for Couples

- Individual growth changes relationship dynamics.
- Fear of being left behind often masquerades as resistance.
- Growth requires communication, not assumptions.
- Couples must update expectations as they evolve.

Lessons for Therapists

- Explore identity shifts and their relational impact.
- Help partners articulate fears beneath resistance.
- Normalise uneven growth as a common relationship stage.
- Support couples in co-creating a new shared direction.

The Parenting Divide

Evelyn walked in stiffly, her arms wrapped tightly around her waist as though holding herself together. Sam followed behind, broad-shouldered but visibly weary, the sluggish movements of a man carrying more than his share. They sat with a cushion's width of space between them, a symbolic distance carved by years of arguing over how to raise their young son.

Evelyn explained:

"I grew up in chaos. I want routines, calm, structure. Sam thinks our son should 'toughen up.'"

Sam shook his head.

"My dad raised us with discipline. It worked. Evelyn babies him. I feel like the bad guy all the time."

Their arguments were not really about parenting styles. They were about the emotional legacies of their own childhoods. Evelyn's softness came from fear of recreating her past. Sam's strictness came from believing it was the only path to strength.

The turning point came when Sam finally admitted:

"I don't want our son to fear me… the way I feared mine."

Evelyn's shoulders softened.

"I don't want to smother him either. I just want him to feel safe."

For the first time, they were no longer fighting each other. They were fighting to become better parents together.

Lessons for Couples

- Parenting conflict is often rooted in childhood experience.
- Understanding each other's fears reduces defensiveness.
- A child benefits from blended strengths, not extremes.
- Joint values matter more than identical methods.

Lessons for Therapists

- Explore family-of-origin influence in parenting styles.
- Help partners reframe conflict as shared care, not opposition.
- Support collaborative parenting plans.
- Emphasise flexibility, not rigid roles.

"Alcohol numbs the drinker, and wounds the relationship."

When Drinking Becomes the Third Partner

Marcus entered with the sluggish heaviness of someone drowning in shame. His clothes were clean but crumpled, his eyes bloodshot, his steps a fraction too slow. Rebecca followed with quiet determination, her face composed but exhausted, the look of a woman who had held everything together for far too long.

Marcus rubbed his palms together.

"I don't drink every day. But when I do, it gets out of hand. I blackout. I say things I don't remember. I hurt her."

Rebecca's voice trembled despite her steady posture.

"I'm raising our daughter alone on the nights he drinks. I'm scared of who he becomes. And I'm tired of pretending everything's fine."

Marcus tried to defend himself.

"I'm not violent. I just… shut down. The world disappears."

Rebecca shook her head.

"But so do you."

Therapy was not about blame. It was about responsibility. Marcus had to confront the truth. Alcohol had become a silent third partner in their marriage.

The turning point came when Marcus, his voice cracking, said:

"I don't want our daughter to remember me like this."

Rebecca nodded.

"That's the first real thing you've said in months."

It was the beginning of change. Not a cure, but a commitment.

Lessons for Couples

- Alcohol erodes trust long before it destroys behaviour.
- Partners carry invisible emotional labour during drinking cycles.
- Repair requires action, not promises.
- Children feel the impact even when parents think they are shielded.

Lessons for Therapists

- Address denial gently but firmly.
- Separate the person from the addiction while still holding accountability.
- Encourage structured support beyond therapy, including GPs, AA, and recovery plans.

- Prioritise safety and stability for the non-drinking partner and children.

Loneliness Inside the Marriage

Emma sat perched on the edge of the sofa, hands knotted tightly together, her shoulders drawn in as though trying to take up less space. Ben sat beside her, staring at the carpet, his leg bouncing with restless guilt. They looked like strangers who had once known each other well, but now lived parallel lives under the same roof.

Emma spoke quietly.

"I feel alone. Even when you're in the room… it's like you're not with me."

Ben exhaled sharply.

"I don't know how to fix it. I work, I come home, I do everything I'm supposed to do. But somehow it's never enough."

Emma shook her head.

"I don't need you to do more. I need you to be here. With me. Not in your head."

Therapy revealed the pattern. Ben withdrew when overwhelmed. Emma reached out when lonely. Each response triggered the other, a cycle neither intended.

The turning point came when Ben finally admitted:

"I didn't realise you felt abandoned while I was still in the same room."

Lessons for Couples

- Loneliness can exist even in long-term relationships.
- Emotional absence hurts more than physical separation.
- Connection grows through presence, not productivity.
- Naming loneliness openly can break the cycle of withdrawal.

Lessons for Therapists

- Explore emotional attunement, not just practical contribution.
- Identify withdrawal–pursuit patterns early.
- Reinforce presence through small but consistent actions.
- Support partners in rebuilding shared emotional space.

The Explosive Temper

Lucas walked in with his jaw clenched, arms folded tightly across his broad chest. His partner, Mia, sat beside him with her shoulders slumped, eyes carrying the exhaustion of someone who had tiptoed around mood swings for far too long. The tension was palpable, heavy with things said in anger and regret that followed too slowly behind.

Mia spoke first.

"When he shouts, I shut down. I can't talk. I feel like I disappear."

Lucas stared straight ahead.

"I don't mean to yell. It just… comes out. I get scared she'll leave, and then I panic."

His confession cracked something open. What Mia experienced as rage was, underneath, terror. Fear of abandonment masked by volume.

Mia whispered:

"I don't want you to shout. I want you to tell me you're scared."

The turning point came when Lucas quietly said:

"I've been trying to control you with my fear. I don't want to be that man anymore."

Lessons for Couples

- Anger often hides deeper emotions such as fear or insecurity.
- Shouting shuts down connection rather than restoring it.
- Vulnerability strengthens relationships more than defensiveness.
- Change begins when fear is expressed without aggression.

Lessons for Therapists

- Explore the root beneath anger rather than focusing on behaviour alone.
- Teach de-escalation and emotional naming.
- Create safety for both partners during disclosure.
- Reinforce accountability without shaming.

When Intimacy Drifts Away

Holly sat with her knees pulled towards her chest, her voice barely above a whisper. Ethan sat across from her, hands clasped tightly, his eyes darting between her and the floor. The space between them felt vast, not from conflict, but from quiet distance built up over years of routine and unspoken needs.

Holly spoke first.

"It's not that I don't love him. I just… don't feel close anymore. I feel like we're housemates."

Ethan winced.

"I thought we were fine. We don't argue. We get on. I didn't realise you felt disconnected."

They were not fighting. They were fading. Their lives had become parallel tracks that never collided. Parenting, work, chores, a kiss on the cheek, then sleep.

Therapy helped them understand that intimacy is not lost in explosions, but in neglect.

The turning point came when Ethan said:

"I stopped showing you I wanted you. I thought you knew."

Holly nodded through tears.

"I needed to feel chosen… not just lived with."

Lessons for Couples

- Lack of conflict does not equal connection.
- Intimacy requires ongoing expression, not assumptions.
- Small gestures rebuild closeness more than grand ones.
- Both partners must feel desired to sustain emotional intimacy.

Lessons for Therapists

- Explore patterns of emotional drift, not just overt conflict.
- Encourage couples to articulate unmet needs safely.
- Highlight the importance of proactive connection rituals.
- Support partners in rebuilding mutual desire and presence.

The Partner Who Needed Permission

Leah stepped into the room first, walking lightly, almost apologetically, scanning the space as if checking for danger. Marcus followed, broad-shouldered and tense, his protective stance so deeply ingrained it had become second nature. They sat together, but Leah's hands remained folded tightly in her lap. The posture of someone who had learned to ask permission before speaking.

Leah looked down as she said:

"He checks where I am all the time. Not because he thinks I'm cheating… but because he worries. He says it's love."

Marcus ran a hand over his jaw.

"She gets anxious. I just want to keep her safe."

But safety had become surveillance. Constant texts, tracking apps, questions that felt like interrogations. Leah was not unfaithful. She was exhausted.

"I can't breathe," she whispered. "If I'm five minutes late, he panics. If I don't answer, he spirals. I don't get to just be."

Marcus insisted:

"I don't mean to control her. I just need to know she's okay."

Therapy revealed the truth. Marcus had lost a sister in childhood, and fear had carved itself into vigilance. Leah was not fighting his love. She was drowning in his fear.

The turning point came when Marcus finally said:

"I realise now... I wasn't protecting her. I was protecting myself."

Lessons for Couples

- Care can become control when rooted in fear.
- Partners must distinguish safety from surveillance.
- Healthy relationships require autonomy and trust.
- Talking about fears prevents them from becoming rules.

Lessons for Therapists

- Explore grief-based or trauma-based overprotection.
- Reframe controlling behaviours as fear responses, without excusing them.
- Support couples in establishing mutual boundaries.
- Teach emotional regulation for the anxious partner.

The Apology That Never Lands

Nadia entered with a weary calm, the kind people develop after years of repeating themselves. Her partner, Joel, followed with his hands stuffed into his hoodie pocket, shoulders slumped, his expression a mixture of guilt and frustration. They sat with space between them, the kind that signals distance rather than preference.

Nadia began softly:

"He says sorry all the time. After arguments, after snapping at me, after disappearing for hours. But nothing changes. I don't want another sorry. I want the behaviour to stop."

Joel shook his head.

"I am sorry. I just... don't know how to fix it."

Therapy uncovered the pattern. Joel apologised quickly to soothe discomfort, not to repair the rupture. His sorry ended the conversation for him. For Nadia, it merely prolonged the hurt.

She said:

"Your apologies feel like sticking plasters on bullet holes."

Joel finally admitted:

"I apologise because I'm scared you'll leave if I don't. But then I freeze, and everything stays the same."

The turning point came when Nadia said:

"I don't want perfect. I want effort."

And Joel, for the first time, stayed in the discomfort long enough to hear it.

Lessons for Couples

- Apologies without change erode trust.
- Repair requires action, not just words.
- Staying present in conflict builds intimacy.
- Progress matters more than perfection.

Lessons for Therapists

- Explore why apologies are used as emotional avoidance.
- Teach the difference between apology and repair.
- Encourage behavioural follow-through with accountability.
- Help the injured partner express needs with clarity.

The Child Who Became the Referee

Sarah entered with a brittle smile, clutching her handbag like a shield. Tom followed, his jaw clenched, a man carrying more guilt than he could voice. Between them sat ten-year-old Oliver, quiet and anxious, his shoulders drawn up as though expecting an argument even in the safety of the room.

Sarah began:

"Oliver keeps stepping between us. If we argue, he tries to stop it. If Tom raises his voice, Oliver bursts into tears."

Tom looked devastated.

"I hate that he feels responsible. I don't want him to be scared of me."

Oliver spoke barely above a whisper.

"I just don't want anyone to be upset. If I make them stop fighting, everything goes quiet again."

Therapy revealed a pattern. Sarah and Tom suppressed their conflict until it erupted, leaving Oliver attuned to every shift in tone, every sharp breath, every slammed cupboard. He had become the emotional referee, sensing storms before they hit.

Sarah cried:

"We thought we were hiding it from him. We weren't."

Tom added:

"I don't want him carrying our load."

The turning point came when Oliver said:

"I just want to be the kid again."

It was the truth they all needed to hear.

Lessons for Couples

- Children absorb emotional tension even without words.
- Arguing is not harmful; unresolved conflict is.
- Children should never mediate between parents.
- Healthy communication models emotional safety.

Lessons for Therapists

- Assess the impact of conflict on family dynamics.
- Teach parents to argue responsibly, not silently.
- Support children in releasing inappropriate roles.
- Help parents rebuild a healthy emotional climate at home.

The Quiet Walkout

Ellen sat perched on the edge of the chair, eyes swollen, fingers twisting the sleeve of her jumper. Tom sat beside her, jaw tight, arms folded, his whole body angled slightly away from her. Not in anger, but in withdrawal. They looked like two people living separate emotional lives under the same roof.

Ellen whispered:

"He doesn't argue anymore. He just walks away. Mid-sentence. Mid-argument. Sometimes mid-day."

Tom sighed heavily.

"When everything turns into a fight, silence is the only safe place."

Ellen felt abandoned. Tom felt cornered. What began as an attempt to avoid conflict had become its own kind of punishment. Therapy helped them see the cycle. Ellen pushed harder for connection the more Tom retreated, and Tom retreated further the more Ellen pushed.

The turning point came when Tom admitted:

"I don't leave because I don't care. I leave because I'm terrified I'll say something I can't take back."

For the first time in months, Ellen's shoulders softened.

It was not rejection. It was self-protection.

Lessons for Couples

- Withdrawal feels like rejection, even when it is meant as restraint.
- Pursuing and distancing patterns feed each other unless named.
- Connection returns when partners feel safe to stay in the room.
- Real communication requires slowing down, not shutting down.

Lessons for Therapists

- Identify pursue–withdraw cycles early.
- Normalise conflict-avoidant coping without endorsing it.
- Coach grounding and pausing skills for heated moments.
- Create structured communication exercises to rebuild safety.

"A couple can survive hardship, but not two different realities."

Two Stories, One Marriage

Nadia sat stiffly, her back straight, arms folded as though protecting herself with posture alone. Her husband, Craig, slumped in the chair opposite, rubbing his temples. They were not angry. They were exhausted. And each believed a different version of their life.

Nadia said:

"He says I'm overreacting. That things aren't as bad as I make them. But he refuses to see the mess we're in."

Craig shook his head.

"She makes everything sound catastrophic. We're fine. We always get through things."

Bills unpaid, promises broken, emotional distance. Nadia saw warning signs. Craig saw temporary inconveniences. They were not arguing about events. They were arguing about interpretation.

The turning point came when Craig finally said:

"I downplay things because I'm scared. If I admit we're struggling, I feel like I've failed you."

Nadia's eyes softened.

"And I magnify things because I'm scared of losing everything."

For the first time, they realised fear, not stubbornness, had been steering the ship.

Lessons for Couples

- Differences in perception can feel like dishonesty.
- Fear often hides behind dismissal or exaggeration.
- Shared reality begins with curiosity, not correction.
- Understanding motives makes compromise possible.

Lessons for Therapists

- Explore the emotional function of minimising or amplifying.
- Ask each partner to narrate the story they tell themselves.
- Highlight how fear shapes perception.
- Build a shared narrative without invalidating either experience.

The Long, Slow Drift

Megan sat angled towards the window, staring out as though trying to remember the woman she used to be. Josh sat opposite, posture collapsed, eyes dull. Two people who had not fought, not betrayed each other, not screamed, but had simply drifted apart.

Megan spoke first.

"We don't talk. Not really. We talk about bins, bills, school runs… but nothing real."

Josh nodded sadly.

"We used to stay up until 2:00 a.m. talking about everything. Now we're strangers who share a house."

There had been no affair. No crisis. No betrayal. Just years of responsibilities, routines, and unspoken fatigue. What hurt most was the absence of anything dramatic. Two people who had quietly become background noise in each other's lives.

The turning point came when Josh murmured:

"I miss you. Not the old us. You. Now."

For the first time in years, Megan looked directly at him, really looked, and saw not a flatmate, but the man she had once chosen.

Lessons for Couples

- Drift happens quietly when connection is taken for granted.
- Emotional intimacy needs deliberate time, not leftover scraps.
- Reconnection begins with honest presence, not grand gestures.
- Small, consistent effort rekindles closeness.

Lessons for Therapists

- Normalise slow-drift disconnection; it is common and repairable.
- Reintroduce structured connection rituals.
- Help partners name emotional needs they have muted.
- Support rebuilding tiny moments of intimacy before tackling bigger issues.

The Hidden Drinking

Eleanor sat with shaking hands tucked beneath her thighs, her eyes red, her voice thin and tired. Tom sat beside her, jaw tight, a man caught between anger and worry. The room felt dense with unspoken truths, the kind that leak slowly into every corner of a relationship until there is nowhere left to hide.

Eleanor whispered:

"It's just a few glasses... here and there. I can stop whenever I want."

Tom looked down.

"I found bottles in the laundry basket, Ellie. And under the sink. And in your car. You're hiding it from me... but mostly from yourself."

Eleanor stared at the floor. Her drinking had begun during the pandemic, a glass at night, then two. Then three. Over time, it became her way to numb stress, then shame. Tom tried to help, then tried to ignore it, then reached breaking point.

The turning point came when Eleanor admitted:

"I'm scared... not of quitting, but of who I'll be without it."

Therapy became a place to name the shame and rebuild trust step by step, with honesty replacing secrecy and companionship replacing coping.

Lessons for Couples

- Avoidance fuels secrecy; secrecy fuels addiction.
- Recovery requires partnership, not policing.
- Honesty is the first step towards rebuilding trust.
- Couples must create shared routines that support sobriety.

Lessons for Therapists

- Explore the emotional function of hidden drinking.
- Help the couple differentiate support from control.
- Encourage consistent, transparent communication.
- Integrate relapse planning as part of long-term healing.

When Sex Becomes a Duty

Maria sat upright, her hands clasped and her smile brittle. A woman who had learned to pretend long before she ever learned to ask for what she needed. Callum slouched beside her, confusion etched across his face, desperate but defensive. The distance between them felt familiar, routine, expected, and deeply lonely.

Maria took a breath.

"I've been faking it for years. Not every time… but most. I didn't want to hurt you. I thought it was what I was supposed to do."

Callum blinked, stunned.

"I thought we had a good sex life. I thought you were happy. How am I supposed to trust anything now?"

Maria's voice broke.

"I love you. But it stopped being about us and became something I owed you. And then I couldn't stop pretending."

Therapy peeled back years of habit. Maria performing intimacy. Callum interpreting that performance as connection. Once the mask cracked, the truth emerged. Neither partner felt wanted, understood, or truly seen.

The turning point came when Callum whispered:

"I don't want a performance. I just want you, even if that means slowing everything down."

And for the first time in years, Maria exhaled with relief.

Lessons for Couples

- Pretending creates distance greater than rejection.
- Honest communication is the foundation of real intimacy.
- Desire grows in safety, not pressure.
- Slowing down can deepen connection.

Lessons for Therapists

- Explore societal and relational scripts around duty.
- Normalise varied libidos and redefine intimacy together.
- Encourage honest, shame-free conversations about sex.
- Teach couples to build trust through honesty, not performance.

Rage as a Defence

Owen stormed into the room first, voice loud, shoulders tight, the kind of man whose frustration filled every space before he even sat down. Maya followed quietly, eyes down, wringing her hands. She looked exhausted, as if living in constant readiness for the next explosion.

Owen snapped:

"She keeps saying I'm angry all the time. I'm not. She winds me up. She never listens."

Maya spoke softly:

"I can't breathe when he shouts. I freeze. I don't say anything because I'm scared he'll get louder."

Owen rolled his eyes, but looked shaken.

"I'm not scary. I'm just... frustrated. At everything. Work. Money. Life. And she's the only one I can talk to."

Therapy uncovered an old truth. Owen had been raised in a house where emotions were met with anger, not understanding. Shouting became his language for fear, overwhelm, and vulnerability.

The turning point came when Maya said:

"I don't need you calm all the time. I just need you safe."

For the first time, Owen cried instead of yelling.

Lessons for Couples

- Anger often masks fear, insecurity, or overwhelm.
- Safety, not silence, restores connection.
- Emotional regulation must be learned, not demanded.
- Partners need boundaries as much as compassion.

Lessons for Therapists

- Help clients explore the function of anger, not just its impact.
- Teach emotional vocabulary in place of reactive behaviour.
- Support the couple in building safety plans.
- Reinforce accountability without shaming.

The Long Silence

Megan entered with her shoulders drawn in, a woman who had learned to walk quietly around conflict. Tom followed behind, heavy-footed, arms folded, the stance of a man who felt blamed no matter what he said. They sat close but stiff, the space between them filled with unspoken hurts that had never been resolved, only stored.

For years, arguments in their home ended not with repair, but with silence. Not peaceful silence, but punishing silence. Days without words, sometimes weeks.

Megan described it softly.

"He shuts down. I talk and talk trying to fix it, and he walks away. I feel invisible."

Tom stared at the carpet.

"When she talks, I feel attacked. I freeze. I go quiet so I don't make it worse."

But the quiet did make it worse. Silence became a weapon neither intended to use, but both suffered from. Therapy traced the pattern back to childhood. Megan grew up in a noisy, expressive home. Tom in a house where feelings were ignored.

The turning point came when Tom said quietly:

"I thought silence protected us. I didn't realise it was hurting you."

Lessons for Couples

- Silence can wound as deeply as shouting.
- Communication needs pacing, not pressure or withdrawal.
- Repair requires naming needs without blame.
- Emotional safety grows when both partners stay present.

Lessons for Therapists

- Explore family-of-origin communication patterns.
- Teach regulated conversation skills.
- Support couples in tolerating discomfort instead of shutting down.
- Normalise slow, structured repair after conflict.

The TikTok Marriage

Hannah arrived immaculate, her phone already open as she checked notifications before even sitting down. Her husband, Paul, trailed behind, hands in his pockets, the look of a man competing with a screen he could never match. They sat side by side, but her eyes flicked constantly to her phone, a glowing presence in the room, as if the third member of their marriage.

Hannah laughed lightly.

"I plan our whole life around TikTok trends. The house, the holidays, even what the kids wear. It motivates me."

Paul looked defeated.

"It motivates her. But it makes me feel like nothing we do is real unless she films it."

Hannah insisted she was just having fun, but therapy uncovered the truth. Every perfect moment was curated, not lived. Paul missed their real life, the messy one Hannah kept editing out.

The turning point came when she whispered:

"I think I forgot I had a life offline."

Lessons for Couples

- Social media can inspire or suffocate a relationship.
- Online validation cannot replace real connection.
- Couples need boundaries around technology.
- Real memories outlast curated ones.

Lessons for Therapists

- Explore links between self-worth and online identity.
- Help partners negotiate screen-use boundaries.
- Encourage realistic expectations, not perfectionism.
- Support couples in re-learning presence without performance.

The Constant Escape

Miles entered first, restless, tapping his foot, scanning the room as if looking for exits. His partner, Layla, followed slowly, eyes heavy with sadness, the expression of someone who had been left behind emotionally too many times. They sat angled away from each other, a couple living parallel lives, never quite meeting.

Miles admitted:

"When things get stressful, I need to get out. I go for drives. I stay late at work. I tell myself it's to clear my head. But it's easier to escape than talk."

Layla's voice cracked.

"He leaves me with all the feelings. I sit alone, wondering what I did wrong. He gets space. I get loneliness."

Therapy revealed a deeper truth. Miles grew up in chaos, where disappearing was the only coping tool he had. As an adult, the habit stayed, but now it hurt the person he loved. Layla did not need constant closeness. She needed consistency.

The turning point came when Miles said:

"I don't want to keep running from us."

Lessons for Couples

- Avoidance creates distance that love cannot bridge alone.
- Emotional presence matters more than physical proximity.
- Stress needs shared solutions, not solo escapes.
- Safety grows when partners stay in discomfort together.

Lessons for Therapists

- Identify escape patterns rooted in childhood.
- Teach co-regulation instead of withdrawal.
- Encourage structured stay-in-the-room conversations.
- Support partners in building emotional tolerance.

When Safety Becomes Surveillance

Emma entered first, clutching her handbag as if it could shield her. She scanned the room before sitting, shoulders tight, every movement careful. Thomas followed, jaw firm, eyes alert, the stiffness of a man who believed he was right. They sat close, but Emma angled slightly away, her body telling the truth her voice was not ready to say.

Emma spoke cautiously.

"He checks my location constantly. If I'm late from work, he rings five times. He says it's because he worries."

Thomas crossed his arms.

"I don't want her hurt. The world's dangerous. I'm just looking out for her."

But Emma shook her head.

"You look out for me… by looking through me. I feel watched, not loved."

Therapy unfolded the difference between protection and possession. Thomas believed fear made his vigilance noble. Emma felt her autonomy shrinking daily.

The turning point came when Thomas whispered:

"I'm scared you'll leave me. Watching you felt safer than trusting you."

It was not malice. It was fear. But fear, left unchecked, had become a cage around them both.

Lessons for Couples

- Care should feel supportive, not suffocating.
- Fear-based behaviours still harm the relationship.
- Trust grows from communication, not monitoring.
- Safety must be negotiated, not imposed.

Lessons for Therapists

- Differentiate protection from control.
- Explore attachment wounds driving surveillance.
- Strengthen boundaries and autonomy within the relationship.
- Help partners build trust without coercive behaviours.

The Secret He Couldn't Tell

Miles entered with his hood up, eyes fixed on the floor, as though hoping invisibility might protect him from exposure. Ava followed behind, her worry almost palpable, fingertips tapping her knee in anxious rhythm. They sat uneasily, a silence thick with something unspoken, a secret Miles had carried too long.

Ava finally said:

"He won't come near me. I think he doesn't want me anymore."

Miles swallowed hard.

"It's not that. I… can't. Things don't work properly. And I'm embarrassed."

Ava's eyes softened.

"Why didn't you tell me?"

Miles had been struggling with erectile dysfunction for months. His silence had turned the bedroom into a battlefield of assumptions. Ava believing she was not attractive. Miles convinced he was broken.

The turning point came when Miles said quietly:

"I was afraid you'd see me differently. But hiding it made everything worse."

Shame lost its power the moment it was spoken aloud.

Lessons for Couples

- Sexual changes happen to most couples at some stage.
- Silence fuels insecurity more than the issue itself.
- Vulnerability restores connection where secrecy destroys it.
- Intimacy can be rebuilt with patience, humour, and understanding.

Lessons for Therapists

- Normalise sexual difficulties and reduce shame early.
- Encourage gentle, pressure-free intimacy.
- Explore the emotional story beneath physical symptoms.
- Support partners in communicating needs without blame.

Supporting a Partner with Depression

Ella walked in slowly, eyes swollen, her movements weighted with exhaustion. Jack followed, hands shoved into his pockets, shoulders slumped. The posture of a man carrying a sadness too heavy to name. They sat with a gap between them that was not intentional, but symbolic, an emotional distance carved by months of silence and survival.

Ella spoke first.

"I feel like I've lost him. He barely talks, barely eats. I'm doing everything and nothing seems to help."

Jack stared at the carpet.

"I don't want to burden her. So I shut down."

Ella wiped her eyes.

"But shutting down is also a burden."

Therapy became a space where Jack could finally speak the numbness he had been hiding, and Ella could voice the loneliness of loving someone who felt unreachable.

The turning point came when Jack whispered:

"I thought protecting you meant disappearing. But disappearing has hurt you more."

Depression did not vanish, but the wall between them finally cracked.

Lessons for Couples

- Depression is an illness, not a lack of love.
- Withdrawal harms connection more than honesty.
- Support must include boundaries to protect both partners.
- Small daily check-ins rebuild closeness steadily.

Lessons for Therapists

- Validate the partner's burnout without blaming the depressed partner.
- Normalise the cycle of withdrawal and pursuit in depression.
- Create structured communication rituals.
- Reinforce that progress is slow but meaningful.

The Partner Who Gave Up Trying

Noah walked in first, shoulders slumped, his eyes dull with the resignation of someone who had stopped expecting things to get better. Audrey followed slowly, clutching her sleeve, her guilt visible before she even sat down. They sat together, but the air around them felt tired, worn out from years of trying, then not trying, then pretending.

Audrey spoke first, her voice shaking.

"I know he thinks I don't care anymore. But I'm exhausted. Every time I try to fix things, it feels like he's already decided it won't work."

Noah stared at the floor.

"I used to try. I really did. But after a while… nothing seemed to matter. Everything I said was wrong. Everything I did was wrong. So I just… stopped."

It was not betrayal or cruelty. It was burnout. Two people who had run out of ways to reach each other, slipping into a quiet stalemate where effort itself felt dangerous.

The turning point came when Noah murmured:

"I didn't stop trying because I don't love you. I stopped because I didn't think I could get it right."

Audrey's eyes softened.

"I never needed perfect. I just needed you with me."

For the first time in years, neither of them was defending. They were finally understanding.

Lessons for Couples

- Giving up often masks fear, not indifference.
- Effort must be mutual; imbalance creates resentment.
- Naming emotional exhaustion allows repair to begin.
- Change starts with two small steps, not one grand gesture.

Lessons for Therapists

- Identify burnout masquerading as apathy.
- Slow the pace of repair to reduce overwhelm.
- Support both partners in rebuilding emotional stamina.
- Reinforce hope without invalidating fatigue.

The Visa Nightmare

Priya walked in holding a crumpled letter, eyes red from nights of worry. Hugo followed, hands stuffed into his pockets, shoulders tense with helplessness. They sat close but did not touch, united by love, divided by bureaucracy. The air felt dense with fear of separation neither had chosen.

Priya spoke first.

"If my visa isn't renewed, I have to go back to India. Hugo keeps saying it'll work out, but he doesn't understand the fear."

Hugo looked frustrated.

"I'm trying to stay positive. But she acts like I don't care. I'm terrified too."

Visa delays, paperwork errors, and long processing times were crushing them. Priya felt unsupported. Hugo felt shut out. Their arguments were not about love, but helplessness.

The turning point came when Hugo finally admitted:

"I keep pretending I'm okay because I don't want to scare you more... but I'm just as scared of losing you."

Priya burst into tears. Not from fear, but from relief at not being alone in it anymore.

Lessons for Couples

- Immigration stress tests even strong relationships.
- Pretending to be strong can create distance instead of safety.
- Sharing fear builds connection.
- Couples must face external stressors as a unified team.

Lessons for Therapists

- Validate the unique strain of immigration issues.
- Encourage vulnerable disclosure from both partners.
- Frame external pressures as us versus the system, not me versus you.
- Support practical planning alongside emotional work.

Caring Turns Controlling

Martha entered briskly, her tone clipped, the organised efficiency of someone who micromanaged because she was terrified of chaos. Daniel followed slowly, leaning heavily on his stick, the fatigue in his eyes betraying deeper exhaustion than illness alone. They sat together, but she hovered emotionally, answering questions meant for him before he could speak.

Daniel sighed.

"She means well. But she decides everything for me. What I eat, when I rest, who I see."

Martha defended herself:

"I'm keeping him alive. If I don't take charge, he'll end up back in hospital."

Therapy uncovered the truth. Martha's fear had turned care into control. Daniel felt imprisoned inside his own recovery.

The turning point came when Daniel said quietly:

"I don't need a nurse. I need my wife. Please let me make some decisions again."

Martha's face crumpled. Not with anger, but with the realisation that her love had started to suffocate him.

Lessons for Couples

- Caregiving requires collaboration, not commandeering.
- Fear often disguises itself as overprotectiveness.
- Autonomy is essential for dignity, even in illness.
- Shared decision-making restores balance and connection.

Lessons for Therapists

- Explore the caretaker's underlying fears.
- Empower the unwell partner to reclaim voice and autonomy.
- Build structured, shared decision-making routines.
- Normalise the identity shifts that come with illness and recovery.

The Slow Drip of Disrespect

Emma walked in with her chin raised but her eyes dull, as if exhaustion had burned away all warmth. Tom followed, shoulders slumped, the defeated posture of a man who had stopped defending himself because he no longer knew how. They sat together, but their bodies leaned away. Two people eroded by tiny cuts rather than one big wound.

Emma admitted:

"I don't shout. I don't scream. But I make little comments… about how he loads the dishwasher wrong, or how he dresses, or his job. I don't even realise I've said them until he shuts down."

Tom stared at the floor.

"It's like being nibbled to death. One tiny criticism at a time. I used to try to fix it. Now I just feel… small."

Therapy traced the contempt back to Emma's childhood, where affection was rationed and perfectionism praised. She judged others the way she had been judged, automatically.

The turning point came when Tom finally said:

"I can handle problems. But I can't handle feeling like you're disappointed in who I am."

Emma cried for the first time in months.

Not because he was wrong, but because he was right.

Lessons for Couples

- Contempt erodes connection more quickly than conflict.
- Small criticisms accumulate into large emotional wounds.
- Respect must be rebuilt through consistency and accountability.
- Safety returns when partners focus on appreciation rather than correction.

Lessons for Therapists

- Identify micro-contempt early; it is often minimised.
- Explore the origin of perfectionism or chronic criticism.
- Help partners name impact without shaming.
- Teach active appreciation as an antidote to contempt.

Anxiety as the Third Person in the Marriage

Sophie sat perched on the edge of the sofa, breathing quickly, eyes darting around the room as if searching for threats. David sat beside her, hands clasped, trying to be calm for both of them but looking frayed at the edges. They held hands tightly, not out of romance, but out of survival.

Sophie whispered:

"I panic if he's late home. I panic if he goes out. I panic if he doesn't text back. I know it's stupid... but I can't stop."

David sighed.

"I want to help her, but I feel like I'm always soothing, always reassuring. I miss just being her husband."

Anxiety had become a third presence in their marriage. Loud, demanding, and relentless.

Sophie was not controlling. She was terrified of abandonment.

David was not withdrawing. He was drowning.

The turning point came when Sophie said:

"I'm not scared of you leaving. I'm scared I won't survive if you do."

It reframed everything.

She was not clingy. She was traumatised.

He was not distant. He was exhausted.

Their work became about boundaries, reassurance, and helping Sophie build internal safety rather than outsourcing it to David.

Lessons for Couples

- Anxiety can reshape relationship dynamics without either partner intending harm.
- Reassurance helps temporarily but can become exhausting long-term.
- Couples heal by balancing comfort with healthy boundaries.
- Internal security, not constant checking, restores connection.

Lessons for Therapists

- Differentiate controlling behaviour from fear-based attachment.
- Teach anxiety-management techniques within the relationship.
- Support partners in setting limits compassionately.

- Frame anxiety as a shared challenge rather than a flaw in one partner.

"Families don't break in a moment; they break in the unspoken years."

The Marriage Surrounded by In-Laws

Holly arrived stiffly, arms folded tight, her smile thin and polite. The kind of smile worn by someone permanently on display. Mark followed, moving slowly, his jaw tense, as though bracing for conflict. They sat close, but the space between them felt crowded with other people's opinions.

Holly exhaled sharply.

"His family comments on everything I do. How I cook, how I parent, how I spend money. They compare me to his ex-wife constantly. And he never says anything."

Mark clenched his hands.

"If I speak up, I'm the bad son. They'll say I've changed. They'll blame her. I'm stuck in the middle."

Holly looked down.

"I stopped going to family dinners. I don't feel welcome. I feel judged in my own marriage."

Therapy revealed a pattern. Mark came from a family where silence kept the peace. Holly came from a family where boundaries were normal. To her, his silence felt like betrayal. To him, speaking up felt dangerous.

The turning point came when Mark finally said:

"I didn't realise that staying quiet meant abandoning you."

For Holly, those words mattered more than any defence he could have offered in front of his family.

Lessons for Couples

- In-law tensions divide couples when boundaries are unclear.
- Silence can feel like disloyalty to the partner who needs protection.
- Couples must stand united in the face of outside conflict.
- Healthy relationships require loyalty inward, not outward.

Lessons for Therapists

- Explore each partner's family norms around conflict and loyalty.
- Encourage boundary-setting as a shared decision, not an individual act.
- Name triangulation when extended family intrudes into the couple's dynamic.
- Strengthen the couple's alliance before addressing external relationships.

The Friends Who Came First

Henry entered looking defensive, chin lifted as though preparing for an attack. Reggie followed behind, hurt written in the slump of his shoulders. They sat as if on opposite sides of an invisible courtroom. One feeling accused, the other feeling abandoned.

Reggie spoke quietly.

"When I plan something for us, he cancels because his mates want to go out. If they need something, he's there in a heartbeat. But for me? I feel like a backup plan."

Henry scoffed, but his eyes flickered with guilt.

"They've been my friends for years. I don't see the big deal. It's not like I'm cheating."

But it was a big deal. Reggie was not competing with infidelity. He was competing with loyalty. With automatic yeses, instant responses, and emotional energy poured outward instead of into the relationship.

Therapy revealed the truth. Henry feared losing his friendships more than he feared losing intimacy. Reggie feared being second best.

The turning point came when Henry finally whispered:

"I didn't realise choosing them meant not choosing you."

Reggie swallowed hard.

"I don't want to take you away from anyone. I just want to feel like I matter too."

It was not about time. It was about prioritisation.

Lessons for Couples

- Friendships enrich relationships, but not when they replace them.
- Feeling second place erodes emotional safety.
- Boundaries with friends protect intimacy.
- Prioritising a partner does not mean abandoning others.

Lessons for Therapists

- Explore identity roles tied to friendship groups.
- Address avoidance masked as social loyalty.
- Help couples co-create shared boundaries around social life.
- Validate the injured partner's longing without pathologising friendship.

When Care Becomes Control

Aisha entered briskly, coat still half on, speaking for both of them before they sat. Rowan followed close behind, quiet and apologetic, his shoulders slumped. They took their seats like a dance they had rehearsed. She leading. He shrinking.

Aisha insisted:

"I'm only trying to help. He makes terrible decisions."

Rowan whispered:

"I can't breathe. She chooses my clothes, my meals, even who I see."

What Aisha called support, Rowan experienced as domination. Growing up in chaos, Aisha believed stability required control. Therapy helped her see that micromanagement suffocates love rather than protects it.

The turning point came when Aisha finally said:

"I thought I was keeping us safe. I didn't realise I was keeping you small."

Lessons for Couples

- Care without autonomy becomes coercion.

- Control often stems from fear, not malice.
- Healthy partnerships need shared decision-making.
- Freedom and love can coexist.

Lessons for Therapists

- Identify control masked as caretaking.
- Explore the controller's childhood narrative.
- Strengthen the quieter partner's agency.
- Encourage collaborative problem-solving.

When Touch Triggers Conflict

Erin sat angled away from Leo, arms folded, skin prickling at even accidental contact. Leo watched her with a mixture of longing and hurt, his leg bouncing, the posture of someone desperate to be close but terrified of causing distress.

Erin explained:

"When he reaches for me, I freeze. I don't mean to, my body just reacts."

Leo replied softly:

"It feels like rejection. Like I'm poison."

Therapy revealed that Erin's aversion wasn't about Leo, but about past trauma she had never disclosed. Her body remembered what her mind tried to forget. The turning point came when Leo said:

"I don't want you to push through it for me. I want us to find a way that feels safe for you."

Lessons for Couples

- Physical withdrawal is often survival, not rejection.
- Intimacy must adapt to trauma responses.
- Consent and safety rebuild connection.

- Patience is an act of love, not delay.

Lessons for Therapists

- Incorporate body-based regulation techniques.
- Validate both partners' experiences without blame.
- Pace intimacy slowly and collaboratively.
- Reframe progress as nervous-system healing, not performance.

Performing Happiness on Social Media

Melissa swept into the room with a bright smile that didn't reach her eyes. Her hair was curled, makeup flawless, her phone already open, as if the session itself might become content. Tom followed slowly, shoulders slumped, the expression of a man who had run out of performances. They sat close, but only because they were used to posing for photos, not because they felt connected.

Melissa said cheerfully:

"If people saw us arguing, they'd think we were breaking up. And I can't deal with the questions. The posts keep things positive."

Tom shook his head.

"We don't talk. We don't touch. We sleep back to back. But every week she posts another picture of us at a café, pretending we're madly in love."

Melissa fiddled with her phone.

"It's just… everyone thinks we're the perfect couple. I don't know how to be anything else."

Therapy helped them face the reality behind the filters. The turning point came when Melissa whispered:

"I don't know who we are without the pretending."

Lessons for Couples

- The online version of a relationship is not the relationship.
- Pretending drains intimacy rather than protecting it.
- Honest conversations build more safety than curated images.
- Connection grows offline, not on camera.

• Lessons for Therapists

- Explore why performative perfection feels necessary.
- Help couples separate image from identity.
- Support partners in tolerating uncomfortable truths.
- Encourage private rituals of connection without documentation.

The Marriage of Avoidance

Ryan entered first, shoulders tight, eyes scanning the carpet as if hoping to find answers there. Emma followed with a long exhale, dropping into the chair like someone carrying years of unspoken frustration. They sat angled away from each other, not in anger, but in exhaustion.

Emma said quietly:

"We don't fight. We don't shout. We just... avoid everything. It's like living with a polite stranger."

Ryan rubbed his hands together.

"If I bring something up, she shuts down. So I stopped. And now we don't talk about anything real."

Their home was peaceful, but only because every difficult topic was buried. Sex had dwindled to rare, hesitant moments. Conversations skimmed the surface. Both were lonely, but neither knew how to reach across the growing divide.

The turning point came when Ryan said:

"I didn't realise silence could hurt more than arguing."

Lessons for Couples

- Avoidance corrodes intimacy quietly but deeply.
- Conflict handled gently strengthens closeness.
- Connection requires vulnerability, not politeness.
- Emotional risk is necessary for emotional safety.

Lessons for Therapists

- Explore the roots of conflict-avoidant patterns.
- Teach skills for safe disagreement.
- Encourage structured communication routines.
- Normalise discomfort as part of relational growth.

Secret Loans and Hidden Stress

Priya strode in briskly, her organised notebook clutched to her chest. She spoke in bullet points, sharp and controlled. Adam followed slowly, the picture of guilt, his shoulders rounded as though bracing for impact. They sat together, but the gap between them held piles of unspoken financial strain.

Priya began:

"I found loan statements. Thousands. He never told me."

Adam swallowed hard.

"I kept thinking I could fix it before she found out. I didn't want to worry her."

Priya shook her head.

"You hid something that affects both of us. I don't care about the money. I care about the secrecy."

Adam had taken out loans to help a struggling friend, then hid the mounting debt. Priya wasn't angry about the finances. She was devastated by the unilateral decisions and the lies by omission.

The turning point came when Adam admitted:

"I was trying to protect you, but all I did was shut you out."

Lessons for Couples

- Financial secrecy is emotional secrecy.
- Joint decisions prevent solitary mistakes.
- Transparency rebuilds trust faster than reassurance.
- Money choices must align with shared values.

Lessons for Therapists

- Explore emotional motivations behind financial concealment.
- Facilitate transparent conversations about money.
- Identify patterns of over-responsibility or guilt-driven spending.
- Support sustainable financial and relational repair.

"A partner's illness affects the body, but it tests the relationship."

Loving Through Chronic Pain

Ellen walked in carefully, each movement measured, a hand pressed to her lower back. She sat slowly, wincing as she adjusted. Mark hovered beside her, anxious, too close in the way of a man who wanted desperately to help but no longer knew how. They sat side by side, fatigue etched into both their faces.

Ellen said softly:

"I hate depending on him. I hate needing help to get out of bed. I don't feel like myself anymore."

Mark replied:

"I don't mind helping. I just miss us. I miss laughing. I miss touching her without her flinching."

Chronic pain had turned their relationship into one of caretaker and patient. Both were grieving the ease they once had, intimacy replaced by logistics, connection replaced by survival.

The turning point came when Ellen whispered:

"I'm scared you'll stop seeing me as your wife and only see my pain."

Lessons for Couples

- Chronic illness impacts identity, intimacy, and roles.
- Communication must expand, not shrink, during health crises.
- Intimacy can be redefined rather than abandoned.
- Shared grief strengthens emotional partnership.

Lessons for Therapists

- Address role fatigue for both partners.
- Explore grief and identity loss tied to illness.
- Encourage new intimacy models within physical limits.
- Teach pacing, empathy, and balanced support strategies.

The Unspoken Resentment

Emma walked in first, her shoulders tense, lips pressed into a thin line. Adam followed slowly, rubbing the back of his neck, avoiding her gaze. They sat close but angled away from each other, the way couples do when they have stopped arguing out loud and started arguing inside themselves instead.

Emma finally spoke.

"I feel like I do everything. House, kids, work. And he just coasts."

Adam sighed.

"I don't coast. I'm exhausted too. I just don't complain as loudly."

It wasn't laziness or lack of love. It was years of unspoken resentment. Emma needed acknowledgement. Adam needed appreciation. Instead, they had given each other distance.

The turning point came when Emma whispered:

"I don't want to keep score. I just want a teammate."

For Adam, something softened. For the first time, he understood she wasn't criticising him. She was asking for him.

Lessons for Couples

- Resentment grows when needs stay unspoken.
- Fairness isn't sameness, it's teamwork.
- Appreciation restores connection faster than criticism.
- Repair requires honest conversations before bitterness settles.

Lessons for Therapists

- Identify invisible labour and emotional imbalance.
- Normalise resentment without shaming it.
- Support couples in naming needs clearly.
- Teach collaborative problem-solving over blame.

The Gaming Addiction

Tom entered with a nervous smile, hands shoved deep into his hoodie pockets. Sarah followed, tight-lipped, her frustration radiating like heat. They sat apart, the tension palpable, the kind that comes from feeling replaced by a screen.

Sarah spoke first.

"He games all night. Sometimes until morning. I go to bed alone. I wake up alone."

Tom shrugged.

"It's my escape. It's the only place I feel good at something."

The problem wasn't gaming. It was the way it had become Tom's identity, and Sarah's rejection.

The turning point came when Tom said quietly:

"I didn't realise the game was swallowing our life. I don't want to lose you."

Lessons for Couples

- Addictions, even digital ones, create emotional abandonment.

- Escapism often masks deeper insecurities.
- Healthy limits protect the relationship.
- Reconnection requires presence, not promises.

Lessons for Therapists

- Explore what the addiction protects or numbs.
- Avoid moralising, focus on function.
- Support structured agreements around technology use.
- Encourage couples to rebuild shared routines.

Opposite Parenting Styles

Amira sat upright, her expression calm but firm. Jake leaned back, arms crossed, the defensive posture of a man tired of feeling wrong. They looked like two people raising the same children in different worlds.

Amira explained:

"I believe in structure. Bedtimes, routines, rules. Jake just… wings it."

Jake rolled his eyes.

"I'm not a drill sergeant. Kids need fun. They need to breathe."

Neither was wrong, but their constant conflict left the children tense and confused. Parenting had become a battleground.

The turning point came when Jake admitted:

"I don't want our kids to feel like I did growing up, scared of making mistakes."

And Amira exhaled:

"I don't want them to grow up like I did, chaotic and insecure."

Suddenly, it wasn't about rules. It was about wounds.

Lessons for Couples

- Parenting clashes often stem from childhood wounds.
- Children thrive on consistency, not perfection.
- Compromise turns two systems into one family unit.
- Unity reduces anxiety for both parents and children.

Lessons for Therapists

- Explore family-of-origin experiences around discipline.
- Help create shared parenting values.
- Normalise differences while avoiding polarisation.
- Support communication that prioritises the children's wellbeing.

Growing Apart in Midlife

Helen entered with tired eyes, her hands folded in her lap. Mark followed, shoulders slumped, the look of someone trying to hold something together with fraying thread. They sat close, but their energy was miles apart, two parallel lives under one roof.

Helen said softly:

"We don't talk anymore. Not really. We talk about bills, the kids, work. Never us."

Mark nodded, his voice low.

"I don't know when it happened. We didn't fight. We just... drifted."

Their marriage hadn't broken. It had faded.

The turning point came when Helen whispered:

"I miss you. Not the old you. You, now. I just don't know how to reach you."

It wasn't a dramatic moment. It was an honest one, and it was enough to begin.

Lessons for Couples

- Emotional drift is often unnoticed until it feels overwhelming.
- Connection requires intentional effort, not routine.
- Vulnerability revives closeness.
- Small daily interactions rebuild intimacy.

Lessons for Therapists

- Normalise midlife drift as common, not catastrophic.
- Coach couples in daily emotional check-ins.
- Explore meaning, ageing, identity, and unmet needs.
- Encourage shared activities that rebuild partnership.

The Quiet Roommate Marriage

Holly sat perched on the edge of the sofa, arms pulled tightly across her body, her posture rigid but her face blank, the look of someone who had forgotten how to ask for more. Dean sat beside her, legs stretched out, looking almost comfortable, as if unaware something was wrong. They looked like two people who shared a mortgage, not a marriage.

Holly spoke softly.

"We don't talk. We don't touch. We barely eat together. I feel like we're flatmates."

Dean frowned.

"I don't get it. We don't argue. Everything's… fine."

But "fine" was the problem. Holly admitted she felt invisible. Dean admitted he thought silence meant peace.

The turning point came when Holly whispered:

"I'd rather you argued with me than ignored me."

For Dean, it was the first moment he realised that quiet wasn't comfort. It was distance.

Lessons for Couples

- A marriage can die quietly long before it explodes.
- Silence is not the same as peace.
- Emotional connection requires intentional effort.
- Naming needs prevents resentment from taking root.

Lessons for Therapists

- Assess emotional disengagement as seriously as conflict.
- Explore each partner's model of peace and connection.
- Support rebuilding small rituals of closeness.
- Encourage discomfort in communication rather than avoidance.

The Fear Behind the Rage

Sam entered with a storm in his shoulders, jaw clenched, fists tight, eyes blazing with defensive anger. Mia followed slowly, her hands shaking as she tucked her hair behind her ear, the way someone does when they have been shouted at recently. They sat apart, the tension prickling the air.

Mia said quietly:

"When he gets angry, I freeze. I don't know which version of him I'm getting."

Sam's voice boomed before he softened.

"I just feel overwhelmed. I'm scared of losing everything. But it comes out wrong."

Therapy peeled back the layers until Sam finally admitted that the rage was shielding fear, fear of failure, abandonment, and disappointing the woman he loved.

The turning point came when he said:

"I don't want to be the thing you're afraid of."

Mia's tearful nod showed him the cost of his outbursts.

Lessons for Couples

- Anger often masks deeper fear.
- Emotional safety is essential before problem-solving.
- Vulnerability repairs more than defensiveness.
- Both partners must feel heard to de-escalate conflict.

Lessons for Therapists

- Separate behaviour from underlying emotion.
- Model emotional regulation tools in the room.
- Validate the partner impacted by anger.
- Support structured communication with safety boundaries.

The Friendship That Went Too Far

Katie sat with her shoulders rounded, eyes swollen from crying. Her husband, Mark, looked stunned, the shock of someone who hadn't expected to be the one betrayed. They sat far apart, knees angled away, two people grieving different things.

Katie whispered:

"It started as friendship. Someone to talk to. Someone who listened."

Mark stared straight ahead.

"You told him things you never told me."

Katie nodded, tears falling.

"I didn't mean for it to turn into… more."

The turning point came when Mark said:

"I can handle the truth. I can't handle lies."

Therapy focused on dismantling secrecy and rebuilding honesty from scratch.

Lessons for Couples

- Emotional neglect creates room for outside connection.

- Transparency must be immediate after betrayal.
- Rebuilding trust requires consistency over time.
- The betrayed partner needs validation, not minimisation.

Lessons for Therapists

- Explore unmet needs without excusing the affair.
- Stabilise emotional safety before deeper work.
- Support structured accountability agreements.
- Help partners understand the stages of betrayal recovery.

Loving Someone Who Never Felt Loved

Eleanor sat folded into herself, shoulders hunched, eyes darting with suspicion, the posture of someone who had learned love was conditional. Her partner, Lewis, looked worn out from trying to prove himself again and again, only to hit walls he didn't build.

Eleanor said:

"He's always trying to help me. But I don't trust it. I don't trust anything."

Lewis sighed.

"I tell her I love her every day. It bounces off like I said nothing."

Therapy explored Eleanor's childhood, neglect, inconsistency, and emotional unpredictability that taught her love was unsafe.

The turning point came when Eleanor whispered:

"I don't push you away because I don't love you... I push you away because I don't believe you'll stay."

Lewis finally understood what he'd been fighting against: history, not her heart.

Lessons for Couples

- Early attachment wounds shape adult intimacy.
- Reassurance must be consistent, not occasional.
- Patience is essential when love feels unsafe.
- Healing requires both partners to understand the past.

Lessons for Therapists

- Work with attachment patterns before behavioural change.
- Normalise defensive responses rooted in trauma.
- Pace the work slowly to avoid overwhelm.
- Teach partners to offer structured, predictable reassurance.

Secrets in the Bottle

Eleanor walked in with trembling hands, her eyes watery, skin pale and tight around the jaw. Tom followed slowly, shoulders hunched, as if already bracing for blame. They sat side by side, but the distance between them felt like an entire year of broken promises.

Eleanor whispered:

"I didn't mean to hide it. I just didn't want him to see how bad I'd gotten."

Tom swallowed hard.

"I kept thinking she loved the drink more than she loved me."

Eleanor had begun drinking secretly, small bottles stashed in handbags, drawers, the garage. Tom found them accidentally, each one feeling like another blow. Therapy became a long, painful unpacking of shame, fear, and the need for escape.

The turning point came when Eleanor said:

"I'm not drinking because I don't care. I'm drinking because I feel like I'm drowning."

For Tom, it was the first time he heard her pain rather than her excuses.

Lessons for Couples

- Addiction is often rooted in pain, not indifference.
- Secrecy is as damaging as the addiction itself.
- Recovery requires compassion paired with boundaries.
- Healing is slow, but shared honesty restores connection.

Lessons for Therapists

- Explore the emotional function of the substance.
- Address shame before demanding behavioural change.
- Help the non-addicted partner set realistic boundaries.
- Collaborate on long-term plans, not quick fixes.

The Scorekeeping Marriage

Robin sat forward stiffly, arms folded across his chest, eyes flat with exhaustion. Maria sat opposite him, knees drawn in, lips tight, her voice laced with a quiet fury she'd grown used to carrying. Every word between them felt pre-weighed, who had done more, who had done less, who had suffered most.

Maria broke first.

"I do everything in this house. Everything. And he still says I'm nagging."

Robin shot back:

"She keeps a tally of every time I fail. I'm sick of feeling like I'm on trial."

Therapy revealed a decade-long pattern, small grudges saved like coins in a jar, ready to be emptied out in every argument. There was no generosity left, only the constant exchange of emotional invoices.

The turning point came when Robin said softly:

"I don't want to win anymore. I just want us to stop fighting."

For the first time, Maria looked at him not as an opponent, but as a partner who was also tired.

Lessons for Couples

- Scorekeeping destroys safety in relationships.
- Repair requires generosity, not perfect balance.
- Couples must trade blame for curiosity.
- Letting go is a skill, not a personality trait.

Lessons for Therapists

- Explore early experiences of criticism and shame.
- Teach couples to interrupt resentment loops.
- Reinforce micro-repairs in communication.
- Help partners value connection over being right.

When Love Feels Like Permission

Nadia entered with her shoulders curled inwards, her hands tucked between her knees, as if she wanted to make herself as small as possible. Callum followed confidently, too confidently, taking the seat closest to me, his arm draped across the back of Nadia's chair as though to claim her in the room.

Nadia spoke quietly.

"He checks my phone. My bank. Where I go. Who I talk to."

Callum shrugged.

"I'm protecting us. She's naïve. People take advantage of her."

Nadia's voice cracked.

"I'm scared to disappoint him. Scared to make a mistake."

Therapy stripped away the justifications and revealed the truth. Callum's control came from fear of abandonment. Nadia's compliance came from fear of conflict. Both were trapped, not with each other, but with their own histories.

The turning point came when Callum finally said:

"I don't want to be the man who scares you."

For Nadia, it was the first time she felt seen rather than managed.

Lessons for Couples

- Control often hides fear, not dominance.
- True safety comes from communication, not surveillance.
- Ease grows when both partners feel free to express needs.
- For change to last, both must confront the fears beneath the behaviour.

Lessons for Therapists

- Identify control patterns early and explicitly.
- Explore attachment wounds driving controlling behaviours.
- Support the controlled partner in reclaiming voice and autonomy.
- Reinforce empathy and safety as foundations for behavioural change.

"Some wounds look like anger, but underneath is fear."

The Rage Behind the Silence

Eleanor sat stiffly on the sofa, arms wrapped around her torso as though holding herself together. Her husband, Grant, leaned forward, elbows on his knees, jaw clenched so tightly that a muscle pulsed near his ear. The air felt charged, not with shouting, but with the quiet threat of it. This was a couple who lived in the shadow of Grant's temper, even on the days he never raised his voice.

Eleanor spoke softly.

"I don't fear you hurting me. I fear your silence. When you shut down, I spend days trying to fix something you won't talk about."

Grant looked away.

"I'm not trying to punish her. I just… don't know what to do with how angry I get."

Therapy peeled back layers Grant had never examined. His childhood was full of slammed doors and fathers who spoke with fists instead of words. His silence wasn't control. It was fear of becoming the man he hated.

The turning point came when Grant said quietly:

"I thought staying quiet was safer. I didn't realise it hurt you more than the anger itself."

For Eleanor, it was the first moment she felt seen rather than blamed.

Lessons for Couples

- Silence can be as damaging as shouting.
- Understanding triggers reduces emotional reactivity.
- Anger often masks vulnerability.
- Repair requires communication rather than withdrawal.

Lessons for Therapists

- Explore the client's anger history and modelling.
- Normalise fear-based shutdowns while challenging the impact.
- Teach regulated communication practices.
- Encourage couples to name emotions before they escalate.

The Pain of Repeated Shutdowns

Melissa sat perched on the edge of the chair, fingers intertwined so tightly her knuckles blanched. Her husband, Alan, leaned back with his arms crossed, gaze fixed somewhere above her shoulder. They looked like two people practising coexistence rather than connection: polite, distant, exhausted.

Melissa exhaled shakily.

"Every time I reach out, emotionally or physically, he shuts me down. I feel invisible. I feel unwanted."

Alan shrugged.

"I'm tired. I've got nothing left. When she asks for more, I feel pressured."

Through therapy, it became clear that Alan's withdrawal wasn't a lack of love, but a response to burnout, years of stress he had never voiced. His avoidance had become Melissa's wound.

The turning point came when Alan said:

"I'm not shutting you out. I'm shutting down because I don't know how to let you in."

For the first time, Melissa saw exhaustion rather than rejection, and Alan saw how deeply his withdrawal had cut her.

Lessons for Couples

- Withdrawal often signals overwhelm, not lack of affection.
- Emotional bids must be understood, not avoided.
- Burnout affects intimacy and connection.
- Reconnection requires pace, patience, and presence.

Lessons for Therapists

- Identify emotional bids and blocked responses.
- Explore stressors outside the relationship that drain capacity.
- Teach small reconnection rituals to rebuild safety.
- Frame withdrawal as information, not abandonment.

When Respect Erodes

Joanne sat angled slightly away from her husband, her eyes sharp with hurt masked as irritation. Philip sat upright, hands clasped, trying to look composed but betraying himself with the tremor in his knee. They looked like two people speaking different emotional languages, and neither had the translation.

Joanne began quietly.

"He used to be ambitious, driven... someone I admired. Now I feel like I'm carrying everything. I'm angry all the time."

Philip swallowed hard.

"I know you think I've given up. But every time you criticise me, it gets harder to try."

Resentment had built slowly, the kind that starts with disappointment and grows into contempt. Philip's depression had eroded his confidence. Joanne's frustration had eroded her compassion. They were stuck in roles neither had chosen.

The turning point came when Joanne, voice breaking, said:

"I miss respecting you. I want to find that again."

Philip whispered:

"And I want to earn it back."

Lessons for Couples

- Resentment signals unmet needs, not failure.
- Respect must be nurtured through effort and empathy.
- Criticism shuts down growth; encouragement invites it.
- Rebuilding requires small wins, not grand gestures.

Lessons for Therapists

- Assess underlying depression or fatigue behind "lack of effort."
- Explore unmet expectations and shifting roles.
- Model compassionate curiosity rather than blame.
- Guide couples towards incremental repair work.

The Marriage Held Together by Politeness

Laura entered with a soft smile, the kind that looked pleasant but never quite reached her eyes. Her husband, Ben, followed with perfect posture, hands folded neatly, the quiet elegance of a man raised to value good manners above messy truths. They sat close, but their shoulders never touched, two people bound together by courtesy instead of connection.

Laura spoke gently:

"I don't think we've had a real argument in years. We don't discuss feelings. We don't talk about the hard stuff. We just… smile and carry on."

Ben nodded, discomfort flickering in his eyes.

"My parents never argued. Ever. Everything was polite. I thought that was what a good marriage looked like."

But politeness had become a barrier, a shield against vulnerability. They never fought, but they also never risked honesty. Problems were swallowed, not solved. Affection became formal. Sex became minimal. Every conversation stayed on the safe side of shallow.

The turning point came when Laura finally said:

"I don't want a peaceful marriage. I want a real one."

Ben looked down, voice trembling.

"I'm terrified that if we start being honest... we won't survive it."

But that fear was the very thing keeping them stuck.

Lessons for Couples

- Politeness can become emotional distance when honesty is avoided.
- Connection requires vulnerability, not perfection.
- Conflict handled with care deepens intimacy.
- Emotional risk is necessary for emotional closeness.

Lessons for Therapists

- Identify conflict-avoidant relational patterns early.
- Encourage safe, structured emotional expression.
- Help clients challenge family-of-origin "niceness scripts."
- Support couples in tolerating the discomfort of truth.

Couples Activities

Activity 1: The Relationship Temperature Check

Purpose:

To help couples identify strengths, tensions, and unmet needs without arguments.

You will need:

- Two sheets of paper
- Two pens
- A quiet space

Steps:

1. Each partner writes down one thing they feel:

   - Happy about
   - Worried about
   - Needing more of
   - Wanting less of

2. Swap sheets silently.
3. Read each other's notes without speaking.
4. Each partner circles one item they feel ready to talk about.
5. Discuss only the circled items using "I feel…" instead of "You always…"

6. End by each choosing one small action they can commit
    to this week.

Outcome:

A calm, structured check-in that avoids arguments and increases
clarity.

Activity 2: The Appreciation Jar

Purpose:

To rebuild connection through daily noticing of the good.

You will need:

- A jar, box, or bowl
- Small slips of paper
- Pens

Steps:

1. Label the jar "Things I Appreciate About You."
2. Every day, each partner writes one appreciation and adds it to the jar.
3. At the end of the week, draw the notes at random and read them aloud.
4. If something feels hard to write, that is the sign you need to write it most.

Outcome:

Couples shift attention from irritations to gratitude, building emotional safety.

Activity 3: The Weekly Debrief

Purpose:

To create a predictable moment each week for connection.

You will need:

- 20 minutes
- Phones on silent

Steps:

1. Sit facing each other comfortably.
2. Take turns answering the following:

   - One thing that went well this week
   - One thing that was difficult
   - One thing you appreciated your partner for
   - One thing you need next week

3. Listen without interruption.
4. Swap roles.
5. End with a 20-second hug to reset the nervous system.

Outcome:

Prevents resentment from building and increases closeness.

Activity 4: The Future Vision Board (Couples Edition)

Purpose:

To reconnect with long-term goals and shared dreams.

You will need:

- Magazines or printed images
- Scissors
- Glue
- Large sheet of paper

Steps:

1. Sit together and discuss what you want life to look like in 3–5 years.
2. Choose images that represent:

   - Home life
   - Health
   - Finances
   - Travel
   - Intimacy
   - Family

3. Build the board together.
4. Write three shared goals underneath it.
5. Display it somewhere you both see daily.

Outcome:

Strengthens teamwork and renews shared purpose.

Activity 5: 10 Minutes of Touch

Purpose:

To rebuild physical connection without sexual pressure.

You will need:

- A timer
- A quiet space

Steps:

1. Set a timer for 5 minutes each.
2. One partner gives gentle, non-sexual touch (arms, shoulders, back).
3. Swap roles when the timer ends.
4. No talking except "softer," "firmer," "that feels nice," etc.
5. End with a hug.

Outcome:

Helps couples reconnect physically and reduce tension or avoidance.

Activity 6: Conflict Scripts

Purpose:

To replace destructive arguments with structured dialogue.

You will need:

- Two sheets of paper
- Pens

Steps:

1. Each partner writes:

   - "I feel…"
   - "Because…"
   - "What I need is…"

2. Swap papers.
3. Read each statement quietly.
4. Respond with:

   - "What I hear you saying is…"
   - "Is that right?"

5. Only discuss after both feel understood.

Outcome:

Arguments become calmer, shorter, and more productive.

Activity 7: The Love Languages Week

Purpose:

To help couples understand each other's preferred ways of receiving love.

You will need:

- Internet access to do a quick love-language quiz
- Sticky notes or a notebook

Steps:

1. Both partners individually take a Love Language assessment online.
2. Write down your top two languages.
3. Create a 7-day plan where each day focuses on one partner's language.
4. Do one action per day (e.g., words of affirmation, acts of service).
5. Swap the next week.

Outcome:

Partners stop guessing and start loving intentionally.

Activity 8: The Couples Bucket List

Purpose:

To bring fun, adventure, and joy back into the relationship.

You will need:

- Paper
- Pens

Steps:

1. Each partner writes down 10 things they want to do together.
2. Compare lists and circle the ones you both wrote.
3. Choose three shared items to complete in the next 6 months.
4. Put dates in the calendar.
5. Take a photo each time you complete one.

Outcome:

Boosts connection through shared positive experiences.

Activity 9: The Shadow Work Sheet (Gentle Couples Version)

Purpose:

To help couples understand their emotional triggers.

You will need:

- Worksheets
- Pens

Steps:

1. Each partner writes:

   - "I am most reactive when…"
   - "This reminds me of…"
   - "What I fear underneath is…"

2. Share only what feels safe.
3. Choose one trigger to work on with compassion instead of defensiveness.

Outcome:

Reduces misunderstandings and emotional explosions.

Activity 10: The Couples Apology Script

Purpose:

To teach meaningful apology instead of empty words.

You will need:

- Pens
- Paper

Steps:

1. Each partner completes:

   - "I understand I hurt you when…"
   - "I can see it made you feel…"
   - "Here's how I plan to prevent this in the future…"

2. Read it aloud slowly.
3. Partner responds only with: "Thank you."
4. Hug for 20 seconds.

Outcome:

Teaches accountability without shame.

Activity 11: The Daily 2-Minute Eye Contact Reset

Purpose:

To rebuild intimacy and nervous-system regulation.

You will need:

- 2 minutes
- A quiet space

Steps:

1. Sit facing each other comfortably.
2. Hold gentle eye contact for 2 full minutes.
3. If emotions arise, breathe through them.
4. End with a soft touch: hand, shoulder, or a hug.

Outcome:

Creates emotional safety and reconnection quickly.

Activity 12: The Relationship Resume

Purpose:

To reflect on how far the couple has come.

You will need:

- A4 sheet
- Pens

Steps:

1. Create sections:

   - "Ways we've grown"
   - "Challenges we've overcome"
   - "Strengths we have now"
   - "What we're learning next"

2. Fill it out together.
3. Highlight three qualities you're proud of.

Outcome:

Increases optimism and team identity.

Activity 13: The Intentional Date Night

Purpose:

To make space for connection without routine taking over.

You will need:

- A calendar
- A budget (optional)

Steps:

1. Pick one night per week for a date.
2. Alternate who plans the evening.
3. The planner chooses:

   - The setting
   - The activity
   - One question to discuss

4. No phones except for emergencies.
5. End the date with one appreciation each.

Outcome:

Makes couples feel prioritised again.

Activity 14: The "What I Wish You Knew" Letter

Purpose:

To share vulnerable truths that are hard to say aloud.

You will need:

- Paper
- Pens

Steps:

1. Write a letter beginning:
2. "What I wish you knew about me is…"
3. Include three emotional truths.
4. Swap letters and read silently.
5. Sit together for 2 minutes with no talking.
6. Discuss only if both feel calm.

Outcome:

Encourages vulnerability and emotional closeness.

Activity 15: Dreaming in Thirds

Purpose:

To create balance between "me," "you," and "us."

You will need:

- Three sheets of paper
- Pens

Steps:

1. One sheet: "Things I want for myself."
2. Second sheet: "Things I want for us."
3. Third sheet: "Things I want for you."
4. Compare gently.
5. Choose one goal from each sheet to work towards this month.

Outcome:

Reduces enmeshment and restores equality.

Activity 16: Relationship Appreciation Questionnaire

Materials Needed:

- Two printed copies of the questionnaire
- Pens
- A quiet space

Instructions:

1. Each partner completes their own questionnaire separately.
2. Take your time. Answer honestly, thoughtfully, and without rushing.
3. Once completed, exchange questionnaires.
4. Read silently first.
5. Each partner highlights three answers from the other person that felt meaningful or surprising.
6. Discuss together:

   - What did you learn about each other?
   - What felt reassuring?
   - What felt emotional or unexpected?

7. Choose one answer from each questionnaire to turn into a planned moment (e.g., recreate your first memorable date, or revisit the thing you first loved).

Reflection/Outcome:

This activity deepens emotional connection, helps couples remember why they chose each other, and opens a safe dialogue around love, memories, and meaning.

Relationship Appreciation Questionnaire

1. What did you think the first time you saw me?
2. When did you first realise you loved me?
3. What did you first love about me?
4. What moments from the early days still make you smile?
5. What do you admire about me now?
6. When do you feel most connected to me?
7. What behaviour of mine makes you feel loved?
8. What behaviour of mine accidentally pushes you away?
9. What do I do that makes you feel appreciated?
10. What do you wish we did more of together?
11. What is one thing you miss that we used to do?
12. What's your favourite memory of us as a couple?
13. What part of our relationship are you most proud of?
14. What's one thing I may not know that you wish I did?
15. What gives you hope for our future together?

Activity 17: The Couple's Lining-Paper Art Project (Floor Canvas)

Materials Needed:

- A long roll of lining paper
- Paints, pens, markers, or pastels
- Tape to secure the paper to the floor
- Optional: magazines for collage

Instructions:

1. Tape the lining paper to the floor so it won't move.
2. Each partner sits at opposite ends of the paper.
3. On your side, draw or paint symbols, shapes, words, or images that represent:

   - How you see the relationship
   - What you bring to it
   - What you need

4. Slowly move towards the middle with your drawings.
5. In the centre of the paper, create a shared space, one collaborative image that represents your "us."
6. Talk while you work, or talk after, whichever feels natural.
7. When finished, stand back and look together:
8. • Which parts blend harmoniously?
9. • Which parts differ?
10. • What surprises you?

Reflection/Outcome:

Couples often discover that their middle ground is bigger than they thought. This creates a visual representation of contribution, connection, and shared vision.

Activity 18: The Weekly Check-In Ritual

Materials Needed:

- Notebooks or phones
- A quiet 10-minute window each week

Instructions:

1. Sit together once a week at the same time.
2. Each partner answers these three questions aloud:

    - One thing I appreciated about you this week...
    - One thing I struggled with...
    - One thing I hope for next week...

3. No interrupting, defending, or solving during sharing.
4. After both have shared, discuss how you can support each other for the coming week.

Reflection/Outcome:

Weekly check-ins prevent resentment, build emotional intelligence, and create a predictable moment of connection.

Activity 19: The "What I Wish You Knew" Cards

Materials Needed:

- Index cards
- Pens

Instructions:

1. Each partner writes 5 cards beginning with:

   "What I wish you knew about me is…"

2. Choose one card at a time to read aloud.
3. After each card, repeat back what you heard, e.g., "What I'm hearing is…."
4. This is not a problem-solving activity. It's about understanding.

Reflection/Outcome:

Creates honest disclosure without defensiveness. Helps partners understand emotional worlds they often assume rather than explore.

Activity 20: The "Love in Action" Challenge (1 Week)

Materials Needed:

- A list of each partner's Love Languages
- Notebook or phone

Instructions:

1. Each partner chooses one Love Language action to perform daily for seven days.
2. Keep a simple log (nothing fancy).
3. Share how it felt to give and receive intentional affection at the end of the week.

Reflection/Outcome:

Helps couples move from intention to behaviour, strengthening connection.

Activity 21: The Future Vision Mapping

Materials Needed:

- A3 or A4 sheets
- Pens or coloured pencils

Instructions:

1. On a sheet of paper, draw four boxes:

   - Home
   - Holidays
   - Finances
   - Relationship Goals

2. Each partner fills in their sheet separately.
3. Compare maps and find where your visions match and where they differ.
4. Create one combined "Shared Vision" map together.

Reflection/Outcome:

Reveals alignment and misalignment, reducing guesswork and preventing long-term resentment.

Activity 22: The "Fights That Don't Belong to Us" Activity

Materials Needed:

- Two pieces of paper
- A bin for disposal

Instructions:

1. Each partner writes down patterns or emotional reactions they learned in childhood (e.g., shutting down, shouting, people-pleasing).
2. Read them aloud.
3. Highlight which behaviours you bring into current arguments.
4. Tear the papers and place them in the bin.
5. Rewrite new conflict agreements together.

Reflection/Outcome:

Creates a symbolic and practical reset to break generational cycles.

Activity 23: The Four Moments That Made Us

Materials Needed:

- Paper or a notebook
- Pens

Instructions:

1. Each partner writes down four key moments:

   - A time you felt loved
   - A time you felt disconnected
   - A time you felt proud of the relationship
   - A moment that changed something for you

2. Share and reflect gently.

Reflection/Outcome:

Builds empathy and emotional understanding.

Activity 24: The "Soft Start-Up" Practice

- **Materials Needed:**
- A recurring issue
- A quiet space

Instructions:

1. Each partner chooses a topic that often creates conflict.
2. Practise phrasing it in a way that starts with gentleness:

   - "I feel…"
   - "My need is…"
   - "What would help me is…"

3. Practise for at least 10 minutes.

Reflection/Outcome:

Improves communication and reduces defensiveness.

Activity 25: Gratitude Jar for Two

Materials Needed:

- A jar
- Small slips of paper
- Pens

Instructions:

1. Each partner writes one gratitude slip per day.
2. Add them to the jar for one month.
3. At the end of the month, read them together.

Reflection/Outcome:

Shifts focus from what's wrong to what's right.

Activity 26: The Repair Ritual

Materials Needed:

- A timer
- Two chairs

Instructions:

1. Sit facing each other.
2. Person A has 3 minutes to express how they feel without blame.
3. Person B reflects back what they heard.
4. Swap roles.
5. End by stating one behaviour each will try to adjust.

Reflection/Outcome:

Strengthens repair skills that prevent conflict from snowballing.

Activity 27: The "Who Am I Now?" Identity Sheets

Materials Needed:

- Two printed worksheets
- Pens

Instructions:

1. Each worksheet contains the following headings:

   - What brings me joy
   - What drains me
   - What I'm proud of
   - What I hide
   - What I need more of

2. Fill out separately, then compare.

Reflection/Outcome:

Reveals evolving identities and deepens partnership understanding.

Activity 28: The Emotional Safety Scale

Materials Needed:

- A scale from 1–10 written on paper
- Pens

Instructions:

1. Each partner marks how emotionally safe they feel in the relationship right now.
2. Describe what would move the score up by one point.
3. Create a plan to improve emotional safety.

Reflection/Outcome:

Gives clarity on needs that often remain unspoken.

Activity 29: The Story of Us (Short Narrative Writing)

Materials Needed:

- Paper
- Pens

Instructions:

1. Each partner writes a one-page story titled "How We Got Here."
2. Include:
3. • First impressions
4. • Key seasons
5. • Challenges
6. • Hopes
7. Read aloud to each other.

Reflection/Outcome:

Creates perspective, bonding, and warmth.

Activity 30: 20-Minute Connection Walk

Materials Needed:

- Shoes
- A 20-minute window outside

Instructions:

1. Go for a walk together without phones.
2. For the first 10 minutes, talk about your day.
3. For the last 10 minutes, talk about something you hope for.

Reflection/Outcome:

Rebuilds gentle, low-pressure intimacy and presence.

www.ingramcontent.com/pod-product-compliance
Lightning Source LLC
Chambersburg PA
CBHW070741030726
47601CB00001B/100